ON THE FLY

Nick Curcione

Baja
ON THE FLY

Nick Curcione

Frank
Amato
PORTLAND

Acknowledgments

Most successful fishing trips are the result of a complex interplay of a variety of factors, some obvious, others quite subtle. Likewise, this book represents far more than the lone efforts of the author. It too is a culmination of numerous influences, only here the magical mix is in the form of friendships that have been forged in more than three and a half decades of fly fishing the salt.

The book is dedicated to Harry Kime for obvious reasons. Harry pioneered fly fishing in Baja. It matters little whether there were others before him. The fact remains that it was Harry who was the leading force in opening the Baja fishery to aficionados of the fly rod.

Two of my East coast fishing buddies made significant contributions to this book. Without a doubt, Bob Popovics is one of the most innovative fly tiers on the saltwater scene today and a number of his patterns have become an integral part of my Baja fly repertoire. A mutual friend is Ed Jaworowski who is equally masterful with both fly rod and camera. I want to thank him for his excellent photography and support. I also wish to extend my thanks to another East coast fishing friend, Kevin Sedlack. The knot illustrations are the product of his talented hand. Jeff Solis and Woody Wood are two West coast fly fishermen with considerable Baja experience who also contributed photos as well as enthusiastic support. For sharing their home on the East Cape, I want to thank Gary and Yvonne Graham. They have been gracious hosts.

The folks at Amato Publications helped make this manuscript a reality. My thanks to Frank for taking on the project and to his gifted editor Kim Koch who eased the pain from some of my tortured prose, and designer Kathy Johnson for giving it style. I think Harry would be pleased.

Nick Curcione
Between the tides on the East Cape,
August 14, 1996

Introduction

6

Chapter I

The Fly Tackle System

10

Chapter II

Making the Right Connection

18

Chapter III

Baja's Pacific Coast Surf Zone

26

Chapter IV

Shoreline Species on Baja's East Coast

36

Chapter V

Baja's Bluewater Bonanza

52

Chapter VI

Baja Travel Tips

70

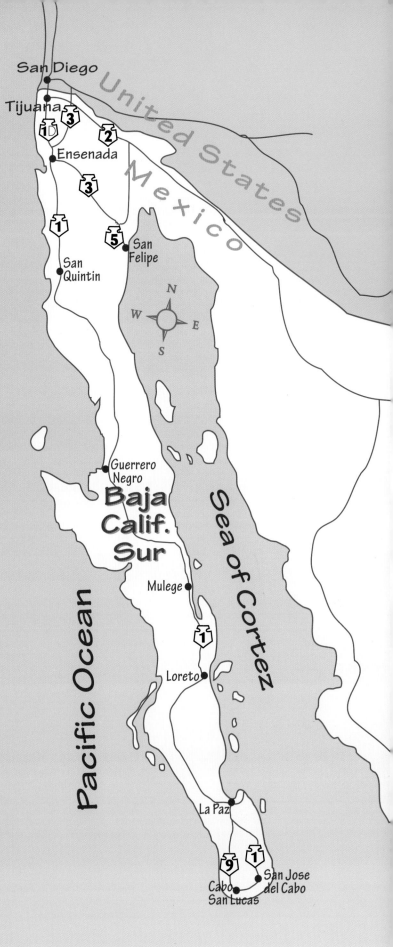

Introduction

The first time I saw a map of Baja was during a geography lesson many years ago when I was in grammar school. Like my grandparents' homeland, Italy, the Baja peninsula was easy to identify. Italy looked like a boot, and to my way of thinking at the time, Baja looked something like a crooked finger pointing south.

More than four decades later that childlike imagery came back to me. I was attending a lecture given by a colleague of mine who is a cultural geographer. One of his areas of specialization is Baja and when he began to discuss this region's geological history, he used the analogy of a finger being broken away from a hand.

Scientists believe that at one point in geologic time, (about 20 million years ago), Baja was actually a part of the Mexican mainland. Mother earth was doing a whole lot of shaking at the time and through a series of volcanic eruptions a chunk of Mexico's west coast was dislodged and the Pacific Ocean seeped in to fill a 700-mile-long crack at the southern end of the San Andreas fault. The resulting body of water is known as the Sea of Cortez.

It is named after Hernan Cortes, the Spanish Conquistador who was the first European to explore this area of Mexico. After he had established rule over the Aztecs in Tenochtitlan, Cortes was still bent on reaping whatever rewards this new land had to offer. Apparently he heard tales of untapped treasures in the Gulf of California and sent scouts into the area. To his delight these rumors proved true because his men returned with pearls. However, these weren't found in any legendary treasure chests like those described in fairy tales. The pearls came from their original source in the form of Mexican oysters. It didn't take long for Spanish royalty to adorn themselves with one of Baja's bounties. Even though a small, local pearl trade managed to operate up until the 1930s, like other fragile natural resources, the treasure dried up quickly. Except for missionary efforts, small mining ventures, scattered ranches and a few fishing villages, Baja was all but forgotten by Mexico, and the rest of the world as well.

No doubt because pearls were easily converted into cash assets, they were exploited early in Baja's history. Fortunately, there are still many natural resources that can still be enjoyed even from a passive sightseer's perspective. Baja remains a land of marked contrasts where nature's designs can border on the extreme. The region has been described as a sea of life surrounded by desert, and if you've spent any time there, the depiction probably doesn't seem too far-fetched. There are sun-scorched dry deserts and volcanic peaks. On both coasts of the peninsula within walking distance of shore, you'll encounter terrain that rivals some of Hollywood's most imaginative set designs. Boulder strewn switchbacks, arroyos studded with cactus sporting spikes like medieval weapons and weathered rock

In Baja, inshore and offshore fishing zones frequently overlap.

*Baja terrain can rival some of
Hollywood's most imaginative set designs.*

ledges resembling artistic renditions of lunar landscapes, are all part of the scenery.

In the gulf itself, there are over fifty islands and thus far scientists have identified over 570 plant species. In this complex interplay of land and sea, there are an incredible number of sea birds and marine mammals that thrive in communities perfected by aeons of evolution. Heermann's gulls, black petrels and major concentrations of the California brown pelican have established colonies throughout the area. The mineral-rich waters of the gulf attract the largest variety of whales to visit any body of water. Bluefin, humpback, Bryde's and sperm whales all traverse these waters.

Of course, of interest to anglers are the finned creatures that frequent this body of water. The gulf is literally a biological horn of plenty, and as testimony to this bounty, scientists have identified 132 different families of fish represented by over 800 different species.

My first trip to Baja was back in 1959. I had moved from the Northeast to Southern California with my family in January of 1957. By today's standards, the fishing in the southland was exceptional. "Log"-size barracuda, big bonito, "barn door" halibut and white seabass in the 50-pound range, were routinely landed from some of the local piers. I thought that it couldn't get any better than this until I met some early Baja aficiandoes who told me about an even more fabulous fishery that was south of the border. These accounts rivaled some of the tales I had read, vividly describing the angling exploits of fishermen like Zane Grey and Ernest Hemingway. The books and magazine articles I poured over as a youth fired my imagination, and now that I was only a two-hour drive from the border, some of this fantasy world of fishing could actually be realized.

My initial exposure to Baja took place on the Pacific side of the peninsula. After promises of better grades in school and more conscientious yard work, my father agreed to take me to Ensenada where we could charter a boat and fish nearby Todos Santos Island. I wasn't fly fishing at the time. Like almost everyone else, I thought that was something only trout fishermen did. Nevertheless, this first excursion into Baja was a memorable one.

There were four of us. My dad, a neighbor friend who had considerable experience in the area, and a buddy of mine. We chartered a 27-foot pocket cruiser and from the moment the skipper dropped anchor, there was non-stop action on barracuda, yellowtail and white seabass. We had live sardines for bait but most of the fish were taken on metal jigs that were cast and retrieved in the clear, bluewater about 200 yards off the island. No one worried about limits in those days and we stopped fishing and catching when we reached the point of exhaustion. For the most part, our conventional outfits with 30- and 40-pound test line were up to the task, but three of the spinning rigs failed miserably. However, luck was with me that day, and I managed to take the largest seabass of the trip on 15-pound test spinning gear. Back at the dock it weighed in at 67 pounds, and 37 years later I have yet to top this fish.

Quite literally I was hooked, and fortunately my parents realized that this was a healthy addiction. Though not to the same degree, my dad also liked to fish, and until I was old enough to drive, he was my main source of transportation down into Baja.

Harry Kime tailing a dorado.

For almost a decade and a half, most of my Baja expeditions didn't extend much further south than Ensenada. First off, the fishing was always so good that neither me nor my fishing buddies felt the need to travel any further. Secondly, from a practical standpoint, roads were few and far apart and no one I knew at the time had a 4-wheel-drive vehicle. That all changed in 1973 when construction of Mexico's Highway 1 was finally completed. The Transpeninsula Highway, "The 1000 Mile Dream," Numero Uno, the roadway goes by all sorts of different labels. My friends and I simply referred to it as the Fishermen's Express.

A Pioneer Baja Fly Fisherman

The early 70s was a formative period in my Baja fishing career. I had returned from a three-year stint in the Northeast where I learned the rudiments of saltwater fly fishing, the Baja Highway was open, and I met and became friends with the late Harry Kime.

From the standpoint of fly fishing Baja, meeting Harry was sort of the equivalent of an aspiring high school quarterback teaming up with the likes of Joe Montana. If fly fishing Baja can be equated with one person, it has to be Harry. I'm not sure if he was the first to actually fly fish the area. That's a moot point anyway. More importantly, Harry was the first to really explore Baja's fishery exclusively on fly tackle. When I met him in 1973, he already had a decade of experience fly fishing the Sea of Cortez. I never had the opportunity to meet Doc Robinson from Florida who was the first to take a striped marlin on a fly off Cabo San Lucas. But here was "Mr. Baja" himself who fought billfish on his own from a skiff and tackled yellowtail from a float tube. I had taken these fish on conventional gear but the prospect of doing so like Harry on fly tackle was almost beyond belief.

Aside from his angling prowess, Harry exuded excitement and when he told you about a particular fishing experience, you wanted to wet a line right then and there. I quickly succumbed to his enthusiasm, and it wasn't long after I met him that I was in his beloved Baja trying to follow in his very large footsteps.

The Organization and Objective of This Text

In keeping with Harry's spirit of sharing his love for the sport with others interested in participating, my aim here is to pass on much of what I've learned fly fishing in Baja these past two decades. In this respect, the book is not a basic text on fly fishing. I am assuming that the reader is already familiar with fly fishing fundamentals. Here, the orientation will be on technique, and the focus will be both locale and species specific. I haven't fished every spot in Baja. That would require several lifetimes. However, I have fished every major area and have taken most of the recognized game fish in the region on the fly. Based on these experiences, I want to provide you with the information necessary to successfully pursue these fish with fly tackle.

Baja has an incredibly diverse fishery so to help organize our discussion, I have tried to break it down into two major zones: inshore and offshore fishing. In addition to the major species in each zone, we'll mention locale, seasons, tackle and appropriate fishing strategies.

Obviously, this distinction between inshore and offshore is not hard and fast. Fish know nothing of boundaries and especially in the fertile waters of the Sea of Cortez, there is frequent overlap concerning which species should be where. A few years ago I witnessed one dramatic example of this when a dorado was caught by a spin fisherman from the beach about a mile and a half north of Rancho Buena Vista. Because of this occasional intermixing of fishing zones, there is also crossover in tackle and techniques as well. For purposes of discussion however, we'll try and maintain the distinction between inshore and offshore fisheries.

Chapter I will cover the fly tackle system. Fly rods, reels, lines (both fly lines and running lines), backing, and leaders appropriate for Baja will be discussed. Knots that you will need to know are covered in Chapter II. Chapters III and IV

Prior to the completion of the Transpeninsular Highway in 1973, Baja roads were few and far apart.

each deal with the inshore fishery. Baja's Pacific coast is discussed in Chapter III, while Chapter IV deals with the Sea of Cortez side of the peninsula, focusing primarily on the Midriff and the East Cape regions. Chapter V takes us into the offshore fishery. The final chapter tells you how to safely travel in Baja.

There are two topics that will not be covered. One involves the rather limited freshwater fishing in Baja. This book deals strictly with the saltwater fishery. The second omission is fly casting.

A Few Notes on Fly Casting

There is no room for argument here. The ability to fly cast is a central requirement for this type of fishing. In fact, it is so important, that I feel it merits separate treatment of its own. A very good book on the subject is *The Cast,* by Ed Jaworowski and an excellent video is "Fly Casting with Lefty Kreh".

Of course, to really learn how to cast, you have to go out and do it. You can't simply read about it or watch videos. However, a word of advice is in order. What you do not want to do is go out and practice your mistakes. Unfortunately, this happens all too often. If you attempt to learn how to cast by yourself, more than likely you'll just end up repeating faulty casting strokes that will be difficult to correct later on. To avoid this, link up with a competent casting instructor from the beginning. Another word of caution: Just because someone is a proficient caster, doesn't necessarily mean they are a competent teacher. There are even some parading around as instructors who cannot cast well themselves. Generally, you can locate qualified instructors by asking around at local fly fishing clubs and fly fishing stores. The regional fishing shows are another good source for contacts.

Finally, once you master the basics, resign yourself to the fact that you will have to continue to practice. Like any physical skill, to stay in top form requires constant repetition. Every good caster I know practices on a regular basis. If you haven't held a fly rod in your hands for months and the time for that long awaited trip finally arrives, it's unrealistic to expect to make good casts the first time the opportunity presents itself. The fishing grounds are not the place to be brushing up on your casting form.

The Fly Tackle System

In the Beginning

With the tremendous surge in popularity that fly fishing has witnessed in the last few years, today as never before, anglers have a wide choice of top quality tackle designed for saltwater. That wasn't the case when I started fly fishing the salt almost thirty years ago.

There were basically only two fly reels for serious ocean angling, the Fin-Nor and the Seamaster. The latter is custom-made and back then it wasn't uncommon to wait at least a year before you could actually get one. Today, in addition to the fine models being offered by a number of major manufacturers, it seems that everyone that has a machine shop is building saltwater fly reels.

Likewise, getting your hands on rods designed for this type of fishing is no longer a problem. In the early days, many of the rod companies were building their saltwater rods as if they were nothing more than larger versions of the freshwater models. The result was that the guides were too small for saltwater fly lines, the reel seats often weren't up to par and some of the fiberglass took a set like a hula hoop.

Fly lines have also come a long way. In the early days, if you wanted a fast sinking line, you had to make your own. That's what Harry Kime did and it opened up a whole new world of fly fishing. It's a totally different story for the present generation of fly fishermen. Fly line technology is expanding so rapidly that it's difficult to keep up with all the latest developments. The same is true with leaders and backing. There is fluorocarbon tippet material and Dacron is now supplemented with super thin gel-spun polyethylene line.

There's no doubt that this constant evolution in tackle development offers tremendous benefit to anglers, but the downside is that it can also get confusing to the point that sometimes you're simply overwhelmed. That's unfortunate, because for many fishermen one of the qualities that makes fly fishing so attractive is that it is a very basic form of angling. You are using a hand line that is cast with a rod. In the following pages I'll try not to lose sight of this fact.

Fly Rods

Most fishing rods serve two basic functions. They have to deliver the bait or lure to the fish, and once hooked, they must be able to help subdue the fish. The first function we all know as casting. In some cases a rod's ability to cast is not really a factor. A big game trolling rod is a good example. Similarly, there are situations where the rod's casting function is secondary to its fish-fighting ability. Many of the bait rods used on party boats and long-range trips fall into this category.

With fly rods however, it's a whole different story. With few exceptions, the fly rod's primary function is to serve as a casting tool. Fly fishing means fly *casting*. If you cannot deliver the fly to the fish, everything ends right then and there. So, regardless of the type of fly fishing you plan to do, the rod has to be such that it can deliver a fly efficiently.

When you venture into the saltwater realm, where the fish are typically stronger and larger than those normally encountered in freshwater, the rod's fish-fighting characteristics take on added importance. Incorporating these two functions into one rod has not been easy, but today's top manufacturers have met the challenge. In terms of materials and design, it is no exaggeration to refer to the present generation of fly rods as true engineering marvels.

Today graphite is the primary rod building material. I still have many of the older fiberglass models but I seldom fish them anymore. In most cases, the newer graphite fly rods are lighter, stronger and cast more efficiently.

In terms of the qualities and features you should look for in a fly rod, the following attributes apply to both inshore and offshore models. First off, all the hardware on the rod including the reel seat and guides, should be top quality. In a saltwater environment, inferior parts will eventually spell failure. The guides should be hard and corrosion resistant. To firmly secure the heavier saltwater fly reels, the reel seat should feature double locking (up-locking) rings. An O-ring between the rings makes tightening and loosening the reel an easy operation.

Unlike most freshwater fly rods, rods intended for saltwater should have fighting butts built in. During the battle stage with strong pulling fish, you'll be sticking the rod butt into your mid-section and the extension will prevent the reel from rubbing against your body. About a two-inch extension is all you'll need especially if the reel seat is an up-locking model.

The rod's grips should feature the highest quality cork. Cheaper grades not only look bad, they'll pit and breakdown in fairly short order. The shape of the handle is also very

In these waters, a fly rod's fish-fighting characterstics are a primary consideration.

important. Most of the saltwater fly rods from top manufacturers have what is referred to as a full Wells or half-Wells style grip. These feature a short indentation for the thumb. The placement of the thumb is very important for good casting technique. In his book, *The Cast*, Ed Jaworowski likens the thumb to a rudder giving directional control as well as helping provide a secure grip on the rod. It is also well established that proper casting form consists of a smoothly executed acceleration of the rod followed by an abrupt stop. The thumb helps achieve this sudden stop, but to do this with maximum effectiveness, the grip must have the proper shape.

A few years ago my friend, John Napoli, who is a champion fly caster, showed me the significant improvement he achieved in both comfort and casting ease by modifying the grips on his fly rods. John deepens the indentation for the thumb and slightly narrows the overall diameter of the rod handle. He does this by sanding the grips using an electric motor with a chuck to secure the end of the rod butt. There are a number of ways to do this, just make sure that the rod turns true otherwise you won't get a uniform contour. If you choose to do this, and I think the end result is well worth the effort, proceed slowly and carefully.

Start with 80-grit sandpaper cut into strips about one inch wide and eight inches long. Grasp the sandpaper strip by the ends and lay it roughly perpendicular to the cork grip. Use very light pressure on the sandpaper. Once you have reduced the overall diameter of the grip, change to 150-grit sandpaper to begin the shaping phase. Periodically stop sanding and grasp the handle to see how it feels. Your hand should comfortably cradle the grip with the thumb resting naturally in the top indentation. Once the desired shape has been achieved, complete the sanding operation by going over the handle a few times with number 600 crocus cloth. This will result in a very smooth finish.

Probably as much a function of tradition as anything else, most fly rods are 9 feet long. Some longer sticks like 9-and-a-half- and 10-foot models see some limited use in wading situations where their greater length makes it a little easier to hold longer sections of line outside the rod tip. Nonetheless, 9 feet is the standard length. Some of the heavier 13- and 14-weight rods are 8 and a half feet. These work a little more efficiently when you have to pump big fish up from the depths. Long rods like some of the 11- and 12-foot Atlantic salmon Spey rods would dramatically shift the leverage in the fish's favor. I don't recommend them for this type of fishing.

Unless you live there, fly fishing Baja entails travel, generally by land or air. That means your fly rods will have to be transported. Up until a few years ago, most fly rods were two-piece. However, today with air travel more popular then ever, manufacturers offer a wide choice of three- and four-piece models that can be carried on the plane with you. Whatever you choose in this regard is a matter of personal preference. The three- and four-piece rods will cost more because of the greater expense in their manufacture, but they perform every bit as well as their two-piece counterparts (in some cases, even better).

Bearing all these features in mind, the two best pieces of advice when purchasing a fly rod are to make sure and select a model from one of the major, recognized manufacturers and to cast the rod before you plunk down your money. As Ed Jaworowski is fond of saying, "one thing about today's fly rods is that they are better than 95% of the people using them."

Aside from the aforementioned construction characteristics, your choice of a fly rod should be governed according to the type of fishing you plan to do. This may sound obvious, but in fly fishing this involves a number of considerations. Not only must you take into account the particular species, you also have to factor in the prevailing conditions. For example, "firecracker" yellowtail in the 5- to 15-pound class close to shore in thick kelp beds involves a different set of demands from what you would encounter with the same fish under a floating kelp paddy miles off the beach. Contrary to what some might expect, the inshore yellowtail normally will call for heavier rods than their offshore cousins. Inshore kelp forests and rock pinnacles, which are favorite haunts of yellowtail, require rods with considerable backbone to help muscle the fish away from this structure. In contrast, an offshore kelp paddy, especially a small one, doesn't pose this kind of problem. There's plenty of open water to play the fish in, and when you don't have to "put the brakes on", a lighter rod can come into play.

The wind and the size of the flies you'll be casting also play a part in rod selection. Casting an 8-weight rod to ladyfish early in the morning when there's little or no wind is an ideal rod choice. In the afternoon when the wind often becomes a factor, you'll find that switching to a heavier rod like a 9- or even a 10-weight makes casting considerably easier. The same applies to the size of the flies you're throwing. At various times the same species can show a preference for different fly patterns. A sleek, sparsely tied fly like a Clouser Minnow will cast fine on an 8-weight rod. That same rod however, will have difficulty tossing a bulky, wind resistant popper. With all these factors to account for you can see why it can be very misleading to say something like, "this is the perfect rod for sierra mackerel or roosterfish."

Having hit you with all these considerations, I'll make the following recommendation regarding rods appropriate for inshore fishing in Baja. Practically every inshore application imaginable can be handled with 8- to 10-weight fly rods. Yes, there are times you can go lighter or heavier, but based on my experience and those of others who have spent considerable time tossing flies in the salt, this range of fly rods is the most practical for inshore fishing. I'm reluctant to recommend one "all-around" rod. Golfers use more than one club and the situation is not too different in fly fishing. Different weight rods serve different functions. Nevertheless, if I were pressed into choosing one rod for Baja inshore fishing, it would be a 9-weight. Better yet, if you can afford two, I would opt for an 8- and 10-weight.

There are a number of situations where a 10-weight rod is a good choice for fishing offshore. I like using it for dorado, tuna and jacks up to about 20 pounds. An 11-weight will also be fine

A rugged, reliable fly reel is a must.

for this size class, but when fish start topping the 25-pound mark, I reach for my 12-weight rod. Over the years, I've taken most of my Pacific sailfish on these rods. The 13- and 14-weight sticks I reserve for big tuna (to me that's any tuna over 40 pounds) and the larger billfish like striped and blue marlin.

Fly Reels

As with fly rods, there is a wide choice of fly reels. In making your selection, exercise the same basic quality concerns that apply to fly rods. At the least, make sure the reel is intended for saltwater use. Beyond that, there are a number of other considerations.

First, the size of the reel should roughly match the rod. Some manufacturers designate their reels according to fly line weights, while others have line capacity specifications. Depending on the type of backing and fly line, the capacities can vary significantly. As a general guideline, for inshore fishing try and select a reel with a minimum capacity of 250 yards of 20-pound backing. For offshore applications, look for reels that will accommodate at least 400 yards of 30-pound backing.

Unlike the case with most freshwater fly reels, those used in saltwater must serve as more than a mere storage receptacle for line. About the only time inland trout or bass fishermen have backing run through their fingers is when they're winding it on the spool for the first time. It's not often that freshwater species like these take you into your backing. However, in places like Baja where the only hatchery is the one provided by Mother Nature, the fish act like pass receivers on the football field. When they feel the hook, they go "down and out". That's why I love this kind of fishing and when you experience it, more than likely you will too. Of course, to derive maximum enjoyment from the experience, your tackle will have to be up to the task. In this respect, when it comes to reels, the most critical component is the drag system. It has to be smooth, and it must be reliable. The simple spring and pawl mechanism found on most freshwater models generally does not hold up well under the line scorching runs of saltwater fish. A disc drag system is far superior.

As a supplement to the reel's drag, I like to be able to apply additional pressure with my fingers or the palm of my hand. A reel with an exposed spool rim affords excellent drag control because you can instantly increase or decrease the resistance manually. In the course of fighting fish I don't like to fiddle with the reel's drag setting. Instead, pressure is applied or reduced by palming or fingering the spool's rim.

Two basic types of fly reels are direct drive and anti-reverse. With the former the handle revolves as the spool turns. In contrast, with anti-reverse models, the handle remains stationary while the spool turns. Anglers used to conventional and spinning reels may wonder why anyone would choose a direct drive "knuckle buster". Admittedly, that handle spinning like the blade on a blender is one more thing to worry about when you have a fish on. If you're not careful, placing a finger where it shouldn't be can pop the tippet and cost you a fish. Worse yet, it can cause some serious damage to your finger. For these reasons, I recommend anti-reverse models to those who are inexperienced in this type of fishing. There is absolutely nothing unsportsmanlike in using an anti-reverse reel and do not think of yourself as any less a fly fisherman if you choose to fish one.

So aside from their long tradition in fly fishing circles, why opt for a direct drive model? The main reason is that it offers very positive control. Even with the drag backed off considerably, when you turn the handle, you retrieve line. There is no slippage.

Another option is that of right or left hand retrieve. The choice should be a simple one. It's the hand that you reel with most effectively.

One additional feature I like for reels intended primarily for inshore use is a quick take apart feature. In inshore waters with the tremendous variety of species and locale, you may want to make complete changes in fly lines and backing and one simple way to do this is to carry spare spools. To be able to quickly take one spool off and pop another one on can be a major convenience. Taking off a spool also makes it easier to clean the inside of the reel and if spool removal is a simple matter, the whole cleaning operation goes a lot easier.

Fly Lines

One of Harry Kime's favorite species in Baja was yellowtail. He managed to find good concentrations of these hard pulling members of the jack family off Loreto and at many of the tiny islands in Bahia de Los Angeles. He didn't have too much difficulty getting them to take his flies when they were chasing bait close to the surface. The problem was that this didn't happen that often. Most of the time the yellows would frequent the depths often a hundred or so feet below the surface. This was well below the range of the fly lines marketed at the time. Well, among other things, Harry was a very inventive guy and he started making his own sinking lines. It was a messy, time consuming process. He mixed a combination of powdered lead and a rubber-based adhesive and applied it to a standard fly line or length of braided nylon. By today's standards, these lines were primitive. Nonetheless, like many of his creations, they worked. I wish I had saved the couple he had given me back then. They're part of fly fishing history and should have been preserved. I

didn't think about that then. Besides, Harry gave them to me to fish and that's what I did.

Today, sinking lines are the primary fly lines for Baja-bound fly fishermen. Just like other sinking artificials that are cast with conventional and spinning tackle, sinking lines enable fly fishermen to effectively present their flies in every Baja locale from the beach to far offshore.

Not only is the fly line the principal item that distinguishes fly fishing from other angling methods, it is also the single most important component in the fly fisherman's tackle system. Of course, you have to know how to cast and you need a decent rod to do so effectively. Bear in mind however, that the fly line has an influence not only on casting distance. More importantly, it determines the depth at which you are able to fish. Let's take a look at both the distance factor and a line's sink rate because both are critical for successful fishing in Baja (and most other places for that matter).

For practically every phase of fly fishing Baja, I see no need for a full-length fly line. Certainly you could fish them, but you'll find that shooting heads are a better choice. When I do use a full fly line it is a specialty type like a Teeny TS. Essentially, this is a one-piece shooting head and running line that offers optimum distance and quick sink rates.

Why is casting distance important? In Baja there are times when you can sight cast to specific fish you see cruising by, but most often you will be blind casting. Here the object is to cover as much water as possible. The greater the area you can work your fly through, the better your chances of connecting with fish. In this respect, the situation is not very different from someone casting artificials on conventional or spinning gear. There are very few instances where these anglers try and deliberately limit their casting distances and neither should fly fishermen. Furthermore, conventional and spin fishermen talk in terms of yards when they refer to casting distance. In fly fishing, distance is measured in feet.

Much has been made of the so-called fact that the majority of fish caught on a fly have been taken at distances of 65 feet or less. This, of course, has never been firmly established. Even if it is true, there are a number of factors to consider. First of all, and this may upset some people, a substantial number of fly fishermen out on the water cannot effectively cast their flies much further than 65 feet. Secondly, until recently the most widely practiced and publicized form of saltwater fly fishing was the kind that takes place on shallow water flats. Here you primarily cast to individual fish that you have spotted and I would agree that in many cases long casts aren't necessary. If you're with a guide on a flats boat, often you can be poled closer to your target. If you are wading, generally it's possible to sneak up and shorten the distance a bit. Likewise, as we'll see in the second section of this book, long casts usually aren't called for in offshore fly fishing when billfish are being teased to the boat. In situations like this you can often get by with a cast that is under 40 feet.

All this notwithstanding, in Baja there are many times when you will need that added distance whether casting from the beach or a boat. When this is the case, the line that will serve you best is the shooting head. Unlike full-length fly lines, the shooting head is designed to maximize casting distance.

A second property of fly lines that is important for consistent action in Baja is the line's ability to sink. I realize that what I'm about to say will raise a few eyebrows. Be that as it may, there is no need for a floating line in Baja. Of course, you can use them and catch fish. But in answer to the question are they a necessity, no they are not.

Like it or not, the fact is that most of the action in Baja is going to take place subsurface. Even when fish are breaking the surface, the commotion you see on top is often the proverbial tip of the

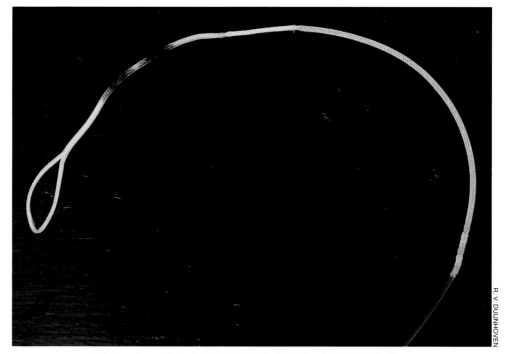

The two long black slashes indicate that this is a 10-weight fly line.

iceberg. Most of the bait, especially those that are injured, are being taken below the surface and this is where you want your fly.

Furthermore, there is no handicap in using a sinking line to present a fly to surface-breaking fish. Fly lines, despite the fact that they may be designated "fast sinking", do not plummet into the depths like a lead sinker or metal jig. Comparatively speaking, they slip below the surface rather slowly. You can even fish poppers on intermediate-sinking lines. Usually, if a saltwater fish is going to hit a popper it will do so rather quickly. You make a few pops with the bug and if nothing happens you lift it from the water and make another cast. Fished in this manner, an intermediate-sinking line will not drag the popper down before a new cast has to be made. If there's a strong current running, (and this is often the case) the line will sink even slower.

So, if you find yourself in a situation where fish are crashing the surface, all you have to do is begin stripping the fly immediately after it hits the water. In most cases it won't be more than a foot or two below the surface and that is well within the strike zone for surface-feeding fish.

There are some additional advantages. For any given size, sinking lines have smaller diameters than floating lines. This makes them easier to cast into the teeth of the wind. The smaller diameter enables you to pack more backing on the spool and it creates less drag in the water. In the section on connections, we'll show you how to put loops in the fly lines to facilitate quick changes.

Shooting lines in a variety of sinking densities are available in most fly fishing stores and catalogues that specialize in this type of fishing. Just like full-length lines, they are labeled according to a numerical weighting system. You will

generally find that if you use a line weight that is one or two numbers higher than the rod's designated weight, the rod will load more readily which makes casting a bit easier. So for example, a good 9-weight rod should be able to handle a 10- or 11-weight line.

When fishing from the shore, I use this overload principle to special advantage. Oftentimes you will find the most productive fishing from steep, sloping beaches. However, this can pose a problem with your back casts. If you're not careful and drop your cast just a tad, the fly will strike the beach, rocks, boulders or whatever happens to be lying behind you. After prolonged fishing you get tired or become a little less attentive and inevitably those back casts start dropping. This happens to the best of casters. Fortunately there's an easy way to handle this problem. All you have to do is use a shooting head that is a few feet shorter than the standard 30-foot configuration. Start with a 30-foot head that is two line sizes above the rated line size of the rod you will be using. For example, if you'll be fishing with a 10-weight rod, match it with a 12-weight shooting head. Then cut two feet from the front of the line and two feet from the back of the line. This leaves you with a 26-foot head that will cast like a rocket on the 10-weight rod. Because it is shorter, it will be easier to work the head outside the rod tip in preparation for your casts, and you'll stand less chance of striking something with the fly in the event you do drop the back cast.

It's important to be able to readily distinguish one line weight from another and a good way to do this is to mark your lines with a waterproof pen. Lefty Kreh showed me this system that makes organizing your fly lines really easy. It's a simple series of long and short slashes. A long slash equals 5 and a short slash signifies 1. For example, if you mark your line with two long slashes, you know it's a 10-weight. If the line has one long slash followed by four short ones, it's a 9-weight.

Lead-core lines are some of the fastest sinking lines you can fish. They also cast like a rocket and are the least expensive lines you can buy. Some are commercially available, but I make up most of my own. Cortland markets a lead-core line appropriately named Kerplunk, and you can make excellent shooting heads with this line. It comes in 100-yard spools and is available in different breaking strengths. For most inshore fishing I use the 27- and 36-pound test lines. Offshore, I step up to the 60-pound test line. It is not the core of lead that contributes to the line's breaking strength. It's the braided nylon over the core. The diameter of the 60-pound test lead-core is smaller than that of most plastic-coated sinking lines. So here you have a very strong line with all the advantages of reduced size.

The best way to go about sizing a lead-core line for a particular rod is to cast 30-foot lengths of line and begin cutting it back one foot at a time until you feel comfortable with it. As a general guideline, 8- and 9-weight rods should be able to handle lead-core lines 20 to 23 feet in length. Ten- and 11-weight rods will accommodate heads 24 to 26 feet long. Though I seldom use lead-core lines longer than 26 feet, 12- to 14-weight rods will handle 28- to 30-foot heads.

Offshore, when I'm casting to fish that have been teased to the boat, I use a setup that Bill Barnes showed me many years ago. Not many anglers do it this way, but I don't argue with success. Bill uses very short heads about 15 feet long. We'll discuss the advantages of this short line in the section on bluewater fishing.

Even in those situations when depth is not the primary consideration, I sometimes opt for a lead-core head. Fishing the surf on the Pacific side of Baja is a primary example. The water turbulence can be likened to a giant Jacuzzi and this can play havoc with conventional, plastic-coated fly lines. They get buffeted about like overcooked linguini. Lead-core lines, on the other hand, are much stiffer and they will track straighter in turbulent water.

Backing

As we noted in the section of fly reels, backing is not merely a filler that cushions the fly line. In saltwater, the backing forms an integral part of the connection between you and the fish so, once again, you don't want to compromise on quality. The old standby is Dacron and there are a number of good brands on the market.

A number of serious big game fly fishermen are beginning to supplement the 30-pound Dacron with the new gelspun polyethylene lines. These are so thin that some of the 50-pound lines have smaller diameters than Dacron lines with almost 75 percent less breaking strength. However, instead of filling the entire reel's backing with these super thin lines, most anglers have found it more practical to top off the Dacron with a couple hundred feet of this line.

Unlike my leader material which I want to be as unobtrusive as possible, high visibility backing like those that are bright orange in color can be advantageous if you have to follow a hooked fish from a boat. It may not come into play that often when fishing inshore, but offshore, for the person running the boat, the bright color makes it easier to keep track of the fish's direction.

For most inshore fishing, 20-pound Dacron is fine. However, in some circumstances when I'm fishing a heavy class tippet like 20-pound test, to gain an extra margin of safety I use 30-pound test Dacron. That's also the case for offshore applications. If anything breaks, you want it to be the class tippet. Otherwise, if it's the backing, in addition to the fish, you'll lose the entire fly line setup.

To facilitate connecting the backing to a running line, I make an end loop in the backing by means of a Bimini twist. The resulting loop should be large enough to pass a reel or coil of line through.

Running Line

The shooting head will require a running or shooting line. There are three basic types to choose from and all of them have their pluses and minuses. None are completely tangle-free, but some are less prone to fouling than others.

First, there are commercially marketed running lines with the same plastic coating as conventional fly lines. They are available in both floating and intermediate density sinking configurations and range in diameter from .025 to .035 inches.

Because of their slick, smooth finish, monofilament running lines have the best shooting qualities. That's why tournament casters use them. They are also the least abrasive over your fingers. On the down side, they tend to tangle more readily, most have a lot of stretch, they are more prone to abrasion, and can break easily if they are nicked.

The running line that I have been using more often lately, both inshore and offshore, is the hollow-core braided mono line. This line seems to tangle less readily than the others and when it does foul, you can often undo the mess fairly quickly. As we'll see, the hollow-core braid construction makes it possible to build strong, smooth connections. About the only disadvantage with this line is that it can really be abrasive on your fingers. For that reason alone, I usually employ a two-handed stripping technique when fishing these lines. One brand that I have had particularly good success with is marketed under the label Elite. It's .043 inches in diameter and is available in 50-yard spools.

Regardless of the type of running line, I always make a loop in both ends of the line. That way I have a loop to loop connection with the backing and a loop to loop connection with the shooting head. In monofilament running lines a loop is easily formed by tying a 5-turn surgeon's loop knot. I learned this from Steve Huff. Steve originally developed this knot for permit fishing but it also works great for mono running lines. With hollow-core braided lines I form loops by means of eye-splices. For plastic-coated running lines, loops are formed with speed-nail knots, a technique I learned years ago from Bob Stearns. All these loops will be discussed and illustrated in Chapter II, "Making the Right Connection".

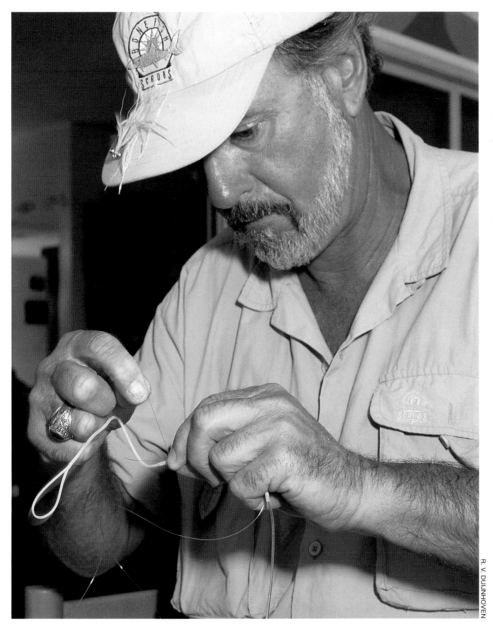

The author rigging a shooting head.

locked with the fly line's end loop. The other loop is interconnected with the class tippet's loop. This loop is formed by tying a Bimini twist in one end of the class tippet. The resulting loop is twisted and folded over itself. A surgeon's knot is tied which results in a smaller double strand loop. Be advised that for IGFA record purposes, the entire unknotted length of the class tippet must be a minimum of 15 inches long.

In many cases when fishing inshore, I don't use a shock leader. The fly is tied directly to the tag end of the class tippet. When a shock leader is used, IGFA standards allow just 12 inches. However, unlike the class tippet, this measurement is not taken from the unknotted length of the leader. Instead, it includes the connecting knots that join the class tippet to the shock leader as well as the knot that is tied to the fly. For example, if the connecting knots are 3/4-of-an-inch long and the knot to the fly is 1/4 of an inch, the unknotted section of the shock leader must not exceed 11 inches. The IGFA recognizes seven class tippet categories: 2-, 4-, 6-, 8-, 12-, 16- and 20-pound test. Not being overly concerned with records and depending on conditions, for inshore fishing I generally fish between 8- and 16-pound test. Offshore, my line classes usually range from 12- to 20-pound test.

On the offshore grounds I do use shock leaders. Except in the case of sharks and wahoo which require wire, the shock leader consists of heavy mono generally from 50- to 150-pound test. Inshore, the one fish where you may want to consider using a wire leader is the sierra mackerel. Even though the IGFA permits a full 12 inches, with that length the fly would never turn over properly. Keep the leaders short, no more than five inches. I prefer single strand wire of about 27-pound test. Haywire twist one end of the wire directly to the fly. At the other end, make another haywire twist to a small, number 7 black swivel. The tag end of the class tippet is tied to the other end of the swivel.

Leaders

The leader system for most Baja fishing can be kept quite simple. When using sinking lines, make the leaders relatively short, about 3 to 4 feet. A long leader defeats the purpose of a sinking line. To aid in turning over the fly, I use a foot-long butt section generally of 30- to 40-pound test mono. The object here is to try and have the diameter of the butt section approximate the diameter of the fly line. Thirty-pound test works well on 8-weight lines. For a 10-weight, I step up to 40-pound test. Offshore where 12- to 14-weights come into play, I use 50- and 60-pound test. For billfish I also lengthen the butt section to about two feet.

A loop is tied in both ends of the butt section by means of a surgeon's knot. One end of the butt section is inter-

CHAPTER II

Making The Right Connection

As the title of this chapter indicates, this is what fishing knots are all about. Especially in saltwater fly fishing, you are constantly faced with the task of joining lines that may differ greatly both in diameter and breaking strength. The trick involves not only knowing how to tie a particular knot, but also being able to select the best knot for the connection you're trying to make.

It would be great if all knots were simple to tie. They aren't, although with practice tying them can become a routine procedure. Some knots are bulkier than others and these should be avoided in places where the connection has to pass through the rod guides.

The most important consideration of all is the knot's breaking strength. Think of the principle of the weak link in the chain. In fly fishing, the weak link should be the class tippet. In terms of IGFA standards, this gives us a range from 2- to 20-pound test. All the other lines in the system, the backing, running line, fly line, butt section and shock leader if you have to use one, should all have a higher rated breaking strength than the class tippet.

As fly fishermen tossing artificial offerings to aggressive, hard-pulling saltwater fish that often frequent "bad neighborhoods", we are already handicapping ourselves considerably by using IGFA class tippets. It would be really foolish to compromise the situation even further by making connections with less than adequate breaking strength.

Whatever the class tippet tests at, the object when tying any knot with it is to maintain its full rated breaking strength. For example, if you're tying a 60-pound shock leader to a 16-pound class tippet, you want to make sure the connection is such that you derive the total 16-pound break limit. In other words, the joining of the shock leader to the class tippet should be what is referred to as a 100 percent connection. Contrariwise, you do not have to concern yourself as much with the breaking strength of the knot used to tie the fly to the shock leader. Say, for example, you use a knot that is rated at only 50 percent of the breaking strength of the line. With a 60-pound shock leader, that would mean that breakage would be reduced to 30 pounds. Nonetheless, there's a big insurance factor here because you are still left with almost twice the breaking strength of the class tippet.

The knots and connections I have selected to illustrate have all proven themselves over the years. That doesn't mean those I have omitted are necessarily poor choices. In many cases, like the Albright or improved blood knot, they are alternatives and many good anglers prefer them. Certainly, there is nothing wrong with knowing a lot of knots provided that you can tie them properly and know when to use them. Many people, including myself, derive a good deal of satisfaction in being able to tie different knots. If you want to learn more on this subject, the best source is *Practical Fishing Knots* by Mark Sosin and Lefty Kreh.

The Basis of the Leader System: The Bimini Twist (100% Breaking Strength)

The Bimini is the one knot that will require the most practice. However learning how to tie it is well worth the effort, because it is one of the few 100 percent knots. The resulting loop is used to make a number of important connections in building a leader system. In one end of the class tippet the Bimini loop is twisted, folded over itself and then tied with a double overhand knot (surgeon's knot). This double strand loop is then interlooped with the end loop in the butt section. Or, if you prefer to omit the butt section, the class tippet can be interconnected with the loop in the end of the fly line. When you have to use a mono shock leader, a Bimini loop is tied in the other end of the class tippet. This will form part of the knot system that is used to join both lines.

For most people, the best way to learn how to tie the Bimini is through personal instruction, but the following steps can help get you started.

Bimini Twist

1. Form a loop in the line, place your hand inside the bottom portion of the loop and rotate your hand making 20 turns.

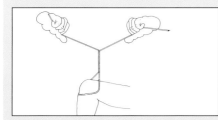

2. Slide the loop over your knee and spread both hands apart to force the twists together.

3A. Grasp the tag end of the line so that it forms a right angle to the column of twists. Pull slightly upward on the standing part of the line (the one with the column of twists in it). At the same time, push slightly downward on the tag end. This will cause the tag end to begin to roll over the column of twists. You can often hear a "click" when it does so. This step is critical. You must effect this initial roll over to tie the knot properly.

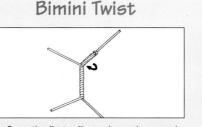

3B. Once the first roll over is made, reposition the tag end so that it is at a right angle to the column of twists. By pulling slightly on the standing part of the line, the tag end should continue rolling over the twists. With the tag end held at a right angle, nice uniform barrel wraps will result. Continue to make these wraps down over the entire column of twists.

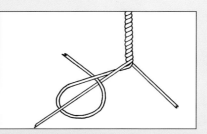

4. When you can wrap no further, grasp the final wrap and pinch it between your thumb and forefinger. With your other hand, take the tag end and make a half hitch around the left leg of the loop. Pull it tight. All the wraps are now locked in place and you can remove the loop from your knee.

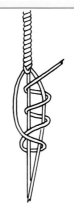

5. Take the tag end and make 4 or 5 turns over both legs of the loop, working back toward the bottom of the column of barrel wraps.

6. Pull the tag end slowly. This will cause the spirals of line to bunch up tightly and uniformly.

7. Snug everything down tight and trim off the tag end.

Connecting the Class Tippet to a Mono Shock Leader: The Speed Nail Knot Connection (100% Breaking Strength)

For years I used traditional knots like the Albright and Huffnagle for joining the class tippet to a shock leader but I've found that this system is even better. You get a smooth, compact connection, even with heavy, 100-pound plus shock leaders. Secondly, because the nail knot's barrel wraps in the shock leader wrap uniformly around the Bimini loop in the class tippet, there is no offset between the two sections. They lie perfectly straight. In addition, the nail knot does not affect the shock leader's breaking strength, so you don't have to worry about tying a light shock leader, such as 40-pound test, to a class tippet of 20-pound test. Here's how to tie it.

Speed Nail Knot

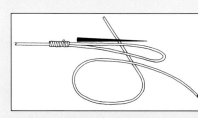

1. Lay a needle or section of small diameter wire alongside the end portion of the class tippet's Bimini loop. Take the section of heavy mono shock leader, form a loop with it, and lay it under the needle. Hold all this together by pinching the Bimini loop, needle and heavy mono between your thumb and forefinger.

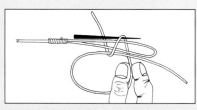

2. Using your other hand, take the right leg of the shock leader loop and wrap it over the Bimini loop, needle, and shock leader. The shock leader loop must pass around both ends of the Bimini and the leader itself to properly form the wraps.

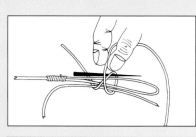

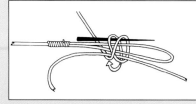

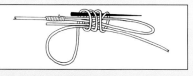

3, 4, 5. Begin forming the nail knot wraps by wrapping the right leg of the heavy leader back over itself, working to the left. When using 50- to 60-pound test leaders, you can make 4 wraps. With shock leaders heavier than that, take only 3 wraps.

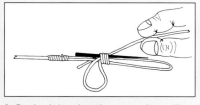

6. Begin tightening the wraps by pulling on the right end on the shock leader.

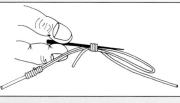

7. Slip the needle out from under the wraps while holding the nail knot and Bimini firmly in place with your right hand. This will prevent the Bimini loop from slipping out through the shock leader wraps.

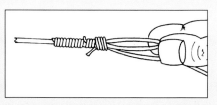

8. Grasp the nail knot with your left hand and pull on the Bimini loop with your right hand to snug the Bimini knot against the nail knot. Finish tightening the nail knot by pulling on both ends of the shock leader. To seat these wraps as tightly as possible, it helps to grab one end of the shock leader with pliers.

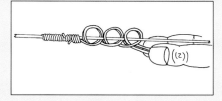

9. Make 3 separate half hitches around the shock leader with the Bimini loop and snug each one up tightly.

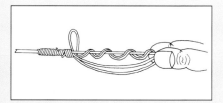

10. Take the remaining section of the Bimini loop and make 4 turns around the shock leader as shown.

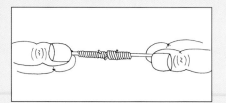

11. Snug this knot tight against the half hitches. Trim the ends of the Bimini and the connection is complete.

End Loops in the Butt Section:
The Surgeon's Loop
(95% Breaking Strength)

The surgeon's loop is one of the easiest knots to tie. As a kid, the overhand knot is probably the first knot you learned to tie. The surgeon's loop is nothing more than a double overhand.

Uni-Knot (95% Breaking Strength)

This is another quick and easy knot to tie. It is a good knot for tying the backing to the spool's arbor. Also, because it will slide, it gives you the option of sliding the knot tight against the hookeye or having an end loop for the fly to ride in.

The Surgeon's Loop

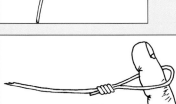

1. Fold the line over itself to form the desired size loop

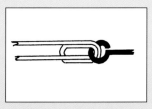

2. Tie in one overhand knot, then tie a second overhand knot.

3. Pull everything tight. A good way to do this is by placing a finger in the loop with one hand and firmly grasping the standing part and tag end with the other hand. Pull both hands apart.

Tying the Fly Directly to the Class Tippet

There are a number of ways to do this. The knot you choose will be based in part on whether you want the fly to ride in a loop or if you want the knot snug against the hookeye.

The Trilene Knot (95%-Plus Breaking Strength)

This knot is excellent for tying flies as well as swivels directly to the class tippet.

Uni-Knot

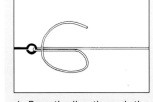

1. Pass the line through the hookeye and bring the tag end back about 6 inches so that it lies parallel to the main section of line. This forms the uni-loop as shown.

3. Pull on the tag end to form the knot. Pull on the standing part to slide the loop to the desired position. If you want to maintain the loop at this position, pull on the tag end to tighten the knot.

2. Make 5 or 6 turns around the doubled line and pass the tag end out through the loop.

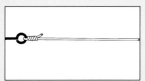

4. Before the knot is tightened, pulling on the standing part of the line will cause the loop to eventually slide up against the hookeye. If you want to snug it tight at this point, pull on the tag end.

Trilene Knot

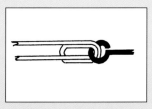

1. Pass the tag end of the line through the hookeye twice.

2. Make 5 to 6 wraps around the standing part of the line and bring the tag end back through the double line loop.

3. You have to take care to draw this knot up properly before tightening. It helps if you alternately pull on the standing part and the tag end. When the knot begins to form, pull only on the standing part.

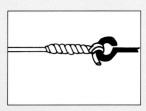

Finished knot.

Non-Slip Mono Loop (100% Breaking Strength)

I believe this knot was first illustrated in Mark and Lefty's book, *Practical Fishing Knots*. With a slight modification in the second tying step, the knot can also be used for tying the fly to heavy shock leaders.

Non-Slip Mono Loop

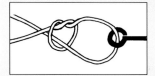

1. Tie an overhand knot in the line and pass the tag end through the hookeye and through the overhand.

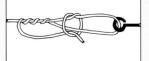

3. Pass the tag end back through the overhand.

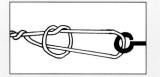

2. Make a series of 5 to 7 wraps around the standing part. Note: when using a heavy mono shock leader, make only 3 wraps. The resulting knot will be easier to cinch down with the heavy line.

4. Pull slowly on the tag end to begin tightening the wraps. To seat the wraps firmly, pull the standing part of the line and the fly in opposite directions.

Steve Huff's 5-Turn Surgeon's Loop Knot (100% Breaking Strength)

As was pointed out earlier, Steve originally developed this fixed loop knot for permit fishing. Well, it also works great on a host of other species. I also use it to form end loops in mono running lines.

Tying a Fly to a Heavy Mono Shock Leader

Since a heavy mono shock leader has such high breaking strength relative to the class tippet, this is one area where you don't have to be concerned with the knot's breaking strength. We already made reference to the modified non-slip mono loop knot. Two other good connections are the Clifford's knot and metal crimps.

Clifford's Knot

Clifford's knot is simply a modification of the time-honored bowline knot used by boaters. It was first shown to me by a guide named Clifford in Costa Rica and in his honor I refer to it as Clifford's knot. Not only is it an easy knot to tie, but it has two distinct advantages. First, the tag end slants downward toward the hookeye. This means that there is less chance for debris to foul on the tag end because it faces opposite the direction the fly is traveling on the retrieve. A second neat feature of this knot is that it's not difficult to untie even after it's tightened. Working the tag end back up through the overhand loop loosens the knot. You can change flies and retie the knot without having to cut the leader.

Crimping a Loop

Technically speaking, a crimp is not a knot in the traditional sense but we include it in this section because it is a very effective means of joining the fly to a heavy mono shock leader. Big game, conventional tackle fishermen have been using them for years. You will need crimping pliers and metal crimping sleeves in the appropriate sizes to accommodate the diameter of the shock leader. When crimping monofilament, be sure to squeeze the sleeve in the mid section. That way, you avoid nicking the monofilament. Crimps are fast and easy to execute, and because there are no knots that have to be drawn tight over a given length of line, the 12-inch shock tippet required by the IGFA for world record purposes can be measured precisely. (See page 23 for tying steps.)

Steve Huff's 5-Turn Surgeon's Loop Knot

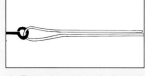

1. Pass the tag end about 6 inches through the hookeye.

2. Using the two strands of line, make a series of 5 overhand knots.

3. By pulling on the loop that is closest to the hookeye, the loop can be worked down toward the fly.

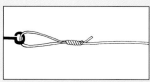

4. To avoid getting stuck, try and grasp the hook with pliers or slip it around a metal ring that you can grab with your hand. With the other hand, grasp the two line sections and begin pulling both hands apart until you get a tight, compact knot.

Clifford's Knot

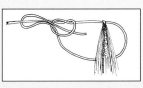

1. Begin by tying an overhand knot in the leader approximately 6 or 7 inches from the tag end. Pass the tag end through the hookeye.

2. Next, pass the tag end through the center of the overhand knot.

3. Now pass the tag end behind and around the standing part of the line and re-enter the overhand knot.

4. Tighten the loop by grasping the fly in one hand and pulling on the standing part of the leader with the other hand.

Connecting Single Strand Wire to a Hookeye and Swivel
Haywire Twist (95%-Plus Breaking Strength)

To join single-strand wire to a fly or swivel, the haywire twist is the best connection. The key to this knot's strength lies in the true "X" wraps that are made in the wire before beginning the barrel wraps. Merely spiraling the tag end of the wire around the standing part can result in the wraps unravelling when subjected to pressure. (See page 24.)

End Loops in Fly Lines: The Speed Nail Knot

This is the procedure I learned from Bob Stearns over twenty years ago, and in all that time, I've never had one of these loops fail. All you have to do is fold the fly line back over itself to form the desired size loop and then bind the two sections of line together with two speed nail knots. The speed nail knot is tied according to the method described for connecting the shock leader to the class tippet. What happens here, is that the mono bites into the fly line's coating and this makes for an incredibly strong loop. To ensure that the mono digs into the fly line, use light line like 6- or 8-pound test to tie the nail knots.

If the fly line has a fairly large diameter, folding the line back on itself can make for a bulky loop and this may have difficulty going through the guides smoothly. To solve this problem, remove about two inches of the fly line's coating. This can be done one of several ways. One method involves soaking the end of the line in acetone for about 30 seconds. This loosens the coating and you can peel it off with your fingernails. If you don't like playing around with chemicals, the coating can be stripped away with fishing line. You can take a short length of 20-pound Dacron, form a girth hitch around the tag end of the fly line with it, pull it tight and then jerk it away toward the end of the fly line. This should strip the coating free exposing the fly line's braided core. Another way of doing this is with a piece of 8-pound test mono. Tie the mono around the tag end of the fly line with a double overhand knot, pull it tight and then jerk it away to strip off the coating.

Fold the exposed braid back upon itself forming a small, half-inch loop. Now tie a 7- to 8-turn speed nail knot around both sections of the exposed braid immediately behind the juncture where the fly line's coating begins. With the loop facing toward your right, tie a second nail knot immediately to the left of the first nail knot. What you want to do here with the second nail knot, is bind the exposed braid to the beginning of the fly line's coating. Cover the nail knots with a flexible adhesive like Pliobond and you're ready to go.

Crimping a Loop

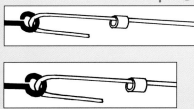

1. Pass the tag end of the leader through the sleeve and the hookeye.

2. Pass the tag end through the sleeve a second time and form the desired loop size by working the main section of leader back and forth through the sleeve.

3. Use appropriate crimping pliers designed to accommodate the size of the sleeve. To avoid nicking the monofilament, crimp the sleeve in its midsection.

Hollow-Core Braid Mono Loop

To make these loops you'll need a simple threading or splicing tool. You can make one yourself from a 12-inch section of 27-pound test single strand wire. Fold the wire in half and flatten the point of the bend with pliers. This will make it easier to insert the wire into the hollow-core braid.

Depending on the diameter of the fly line, you'll need a 12-inch length of 30- or 50-pound test braided mono. Insert the folded end of the wire loop into the braid approximately 6 inches from the tag end. Push the wire inside the braid about one and a half inches. Then push the wire out through the braid. Catch the tag end of the braid inside the wire loop and pull it down through the same inch-and-a-half section of braid. Pull the wire tool and the tag end out through the braid. Carefully pull on this tag end until you

Haywire Twist

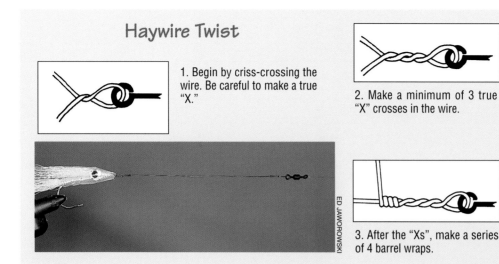

1. Begin by criss-crossing the wire. Be careful to make a true "X."

2. Make a minimum of 3 true "X" crosses in the wire.

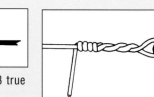

ED JAWOROWSKI

4. Do not cut the tag end of the wire because this will leave a sharp edge that can cause injury. Instead, form a "crank handle" in the tag end of the wire. Bend this "handle" opposite the wraps and the wire should break off cleanly.

3. After the "Xs", make a series of 4 barrel wraps.

have a loop that is from 1/2 to 3/4 inches long. For extra security, I like to work the wire into the braid a second time. Approximately an inch or so below the point where the tag end of the braid was pulled out from the center of the braid, insert the wire and push it up through the braid to the point where the tag end is sticking out. Catch the remaining tag end and pull it down through this section of braid. If a tiny section of the tag end sticks out from the braid, gently pull on one of the legs of the loop until it is drawn completely inside the center of the braid. You now have a double eye-splice.

There should be about five inches of braided line remaining after you have formed the loop. This is more than enough to securely encase the fly line. Cut the end of the fly line on a bias to make it easier to snake into the center of the braid. Slowly work the braid over the fly line using an inch-worm sort of motion. During the process a few strands of the braid at the tag end where the fly line was first inserted will separate. Not to worry. These can be secured after the fly line is worked all the way up the braid to the bottom of the

juncture of the eye-splice loop. Wrap over the loose ends of braid with fly tying thread and a bobbin and whip finish the thread.

After the fly line is securely encased in the braid, tie a speed nail knot with 6- to 8-pound test mono immediately above the point where you whip finished the strands of braid with fly tying thread. Snug the knot so that it digs slightly into the fly line's coating. Coat the nail knot and thread with Pliobond, let it dry and go fishing.

End Loops in Lead-Core Line

As the name implies, lead-core line is simply a lead filament encased in a Dacron shell. This makes possible several methods of making end loops. One very simple technique is to work out about five inches of the lead from the braid. This is done by alternately pushing down on the braid and gently pulling up on the exposed lead filament. Break off the lead filament. Now all you have to do is fold the braid back over itself, forming a loop, and tie a surgeon's loop in the braid.

At times this can make for a bulky loop. An alternative

End Loops in Lead-Core Line

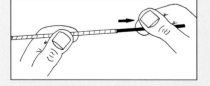

1. Alternately push down on the braided sheath while gently pulling on the exposed core of lead. Break off about 5-inches of the lead-core.

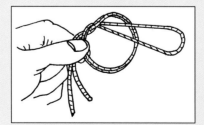

2. Fold the core-less braid back over itself to form a loop and tie a single overhand knot.

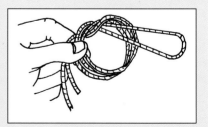

3. Tie a second overhand and tighten the knot using both hands by simultaneously pulling the standing part/tag end and the loop in opposite directions.

Hollow-Core Braid Mono Loop

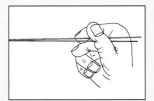

1. A splicing tool can easily be made from a 12-inch length of 27-pound test single strand wire. Fold the wire in half. Flatten the base of the bend with pliers. This will make it easier to insert the wire into the braid.

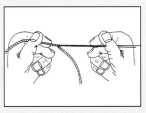

2. Insert the flattened end of the wire loop into the braid approximately 6 inches from the tag end.

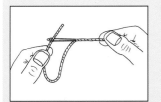

3. Work the wire inside the braid about 1 1/2 inches. Then push the wire out through the braid. Catch the tag end of the braid inside the wire loop.

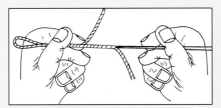

4. Pull the wire loop and tag end back down through this same section of braid. Carefully pull on the tag end to form the desired size loop (1 1/2 to 3/4 inches in length).

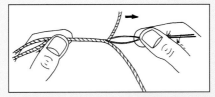

5. For added security, work the wire into the braid a second time approximately one inch below the point where the tag end was pulled out from the braid.

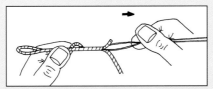

6. Push the wire up through the braid to a point immediately below the juncture where the tag end is protruding. Catch the tag end with the wire and pull it down through this second section of braid. If a small section of the tag end still protrudes from the braid, gently pull on one of the legs of the braided loop until the tag is drawn completely inside the braid.

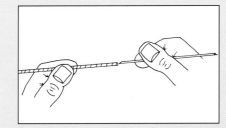

7. To facilitate working the fly line into the remaining section of braid, cut the tag end of the line on a bias.

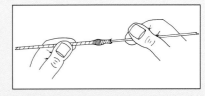

8. Work the braid over the fly line "inchworm style" by alternately pushing and pulling on the braid causing it to bulge and contract. Work the fly line into the braid all the way to the point where the tag end of the loop lies encased in the braid.

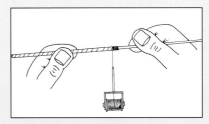

9. Secure the loosened ends of the strands of braid with fly tying thread and a bobbin. Whip finish the thread.

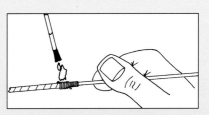

10. Tie a speed nail knot with 6- to 8-pound test mono around the braid in front of the whip finished thread. For a smooth, snag-free connection, coat the nail knot and thread with Pliobond.

that makes for a perfectly smooth loop is the eye-splice previously described. Work out enough lead so that you can make an eye-splice loop in the remaining hollow-core shell.

With some brands of lead-core, the braid is too tight and you won't be able to effect an eye-splice. The alternative is to use speed nail knots to bind the two sections together. Most lead-core is uncoated so you don't have to remove anything except a section of the lead filament. With the lead removed, follow the same procedure described for speed nail knot fly line loops.

CHAPTER III

Baja's Pacific Coast Surf Zone

In Baja, resort development and fishing go hand in hand. Most of the developed fishing resorts are located in the central and southern regions on the Sea of Cortez side of the peninsula. The Pacific Coast is considerably colder. In the summer months when the temperature can be in the high 90s just a mile or so inland, on the coast it can be comparatively chilly in the 70s. The coastal water conditions are also very different. On the Pacific side you have considerable surf and many of the spots require a 4-wheel-drive vehicle. Perhaps that's why there are fewer resorts on this side of the peninsula.

However, all this is about to change. There are six new marinas being developed in Baja's North Pacific zone between Tijuana and San Quintin including four new facilities in Ensenada that will serve private boaters and fishermen. In addition to the surf zone species we'll cover in this section, the principal game fish in these waters that fly fishermen can target are yellowtail and yellowfin tuna. Because these fish have been more accessible in other parts of Baja, they will be discussed in Chapters IV and V.

Ensenada, which is about 70 miles south of Tijuana, is Baja's third largest city, with many hotels and trailer parks. Before the highway was completed, this was about as far south as most tourists ventured. In general, the surf fishing here is better than what you can normally expect along Southern California beaches, but for the best action, plan on

ED JAWOROWSKI

Fly fishing the surf zone is a challenging endeavor.

heading further south. Another 125 miles down Highway 1 will put you into San Quintin where the best surf action really begins. This is a growing resort area with a number of motels and a few trailer parks. You can find good lodging at the Chavez Motel, Cielito Lindo, Ernestos, La Pinta and the Old Mill (Molino Viejo). The further south you travel along the coast, the fewer the accommodations, so if you want to fish this area, plan on camping and bring everything you'll need. Even today, it is a region that has received only scant attention from fly fishermen, but fishing opportunities abound for the feather merchant.

At first glance, plodding into any kind of surf with fly gear may seem about as promising as winning a *grand prix* in the family car. The conditions often appear downright inhospitable. Waves that have pounded the shore from time immemorial have transformed jagged rocks into bowling ball smoothness. If there are errant surfers in the area, their boards get tossed about like pencil poppers. The force of the undertow can make it seem like you're being sucked seaward by a giant vacuum. Add to this the nemesis of fly fishermen, the wind. Particularly when you're trying to fish an afternoon tide, the wind blows in your face with a force that makes you think you're standing behind a jet revving for takeoff.

Despite its formidable conditions, the surf, particularly the Pacific surf off Baja, has an attraction that keeps drawing me back. A frothing foam meandering along miles of open, uncluttered beachfront is a magnificent setting in its own right. And there are fish out there that will take your flies. The experience of a throbbing predator battling you in the middle of a boiling surf is a sensational feeling.

The old adage that the best time to go fishing is whenever you have the time, may be sage advice for people with tight schedules. However, the periods of optimum productivity, particularly in the surf zone, are closely tied to tidal phases. Tidal currents have a considerable effect on the fish's food source. Incoming and strong spring tides (the latter occur when the earth, moon, and sun are in alignment, causing maximum gravitational pull) churn up the bottom, stirring up food sources like sand crabs. In rocky areas, the increased wave action can knock loose a variety of crustaceans and other marine organisms.

Nature programmed larger predator fish to tune in to these conditions. That's why you'll consistently experience the best action on incoming and outgoing tides. An hour before and an hour after the peak high tides are optimum periods. During high-water and low-water slack periods, there's minimum water movement. For the most part, fishing is usually very slow.

Reading the Surf

To the uninitiated, most stretches of beach may look relatively the same. Surfers and experienced surf fishermen know this is not the case. Not unlike the situation that prevails with their freshwater counterparts, the behavior of fish in the surf zone is intimately related to the physical makeup of their environment. As we'll see, this is true for the Sea of Cortez side of the peninsula as well. Some stretches of coast will harbor concentrations of fish while others can be like the proverbial Dead Sea.

Basically, learning to read the surf involves the ability to closely monitor the characteristics of waves as they roll in toward shore. This wave action gives you a good idea of what the configuration of the bottom is like. The key to all this is a principle you probably learned in a high school science class. Waves break over shallow areas. In contrast, they tend to roll over deeper depressions or troughs in the bottom. Therefore, the behavior of a wall of water as it makes its way toward shore, is a good indication of the type of bottom contour that lies below. If you observe what appears to be a relatively flat area of water with waves breaking on either side of it, it's a safe bet that this area is a deeper pocket of water.

This is where you want to be casting your flies. Marine creatures like crabs, worms, and small baitfish are unable to buck the strong tidal currents. Eventually they get swept into the calmer water that is found in these deeper areas. As part of their genetic script, predator fish like perch, corbina, halibut and bass, are aware of this. They establish feeding stations in these bottom depressions. Somewhat like a trout establishing a holding pattern behind a rock or undercut bank where there's a break in the current, surf-zone species frequent the deeper pockets where the water is less turbulent. In places like these, they don't have to expend a great deal of energy just to maintain their position.

Barred perch—surf zone turbos.

As waves roll toward shore, they begin to break. By observing the distance of the break from the shoreline, you can get an idea of the degree of slope that characterizes a particular stretch of beach. On steeply sloping beaches, waves break practically at the water's edge. There will be deep troughs close to the beach, sometimes not more than 20 feet or so from where the water laps the sand. The water here will also tend to be darker in color. It's in these troughs between cresting waves that you want to place

Perch and corbina flies do not have to be exact replicas of mole crabs. The fly at the top center is a Sandcrab Light Pattern.

your casts. Generally, these zones are less than 100 feet off the beach, but with a fly rod you often have to make some good casts.

The surf zone is very different from inland waterways where changes tend to be gradual. Due to the influence of variables like tide, current, and ocean storms, the shoreline is in a constant state of transition. The bottom contour is continuously altered by pounding waves creating new holes and depressions. This means that an area that was productive one day, may not be as good the next. So avoid getting locked into one particular location. Instead, try to cover long stretches of beach in search of congregating fish. Because most of these surf zone species tend to travel in schools, once you get a strike, work the area over thoroughly before moving on. In contrast to bait fishermen who generally stick to a single spot, fly fishermen can better their chances by constantly staying on the move. Especially if at first you don't feel confident in your ability to read the surf, you'll increase the likelihood of eventually hitting productive areas by making a cast and then moving a few yards up or down the beach, repeating the process as you go along.

Barred Perch, Corbina, and Croaker

Consistently, the two most readily accessible species for the fly fisher are the barred perch and corbina. However, if you're at the right place at the right time, yellowfin croaker, halibut, calico and even white seabass can be taken from the surf on fly tackle.

A close relative to the barred perch is the walleye perch and you often find them in the same surf zones. As their name implies, walleyes are distinguished by their considerably larger black eyes. They also have silver sides which are unadorned with the vertical bands found on barred perch.

I like to think of barred perch as turbo-charged versions of freshwater bluegill. They resemble bluegill both in body configuration and the tenacity with which they take flies. The similarity ends there. Barred perch are more powerful. Considering the demanding environment they call home, they have to be. With the exception of river rapids, there are few if any conditions in freshwater that can rival the water turbulence of the surf. A feeding pattern that has them routinely darting in and out of the receding wash between breaking waves requires tremendous reserves of energy. Nature saw fit to program them accordingly as you'll discover when one smacks your fly with a strike that is anything but subtle. Given the nature of their environment, perch don't have much time to deliberate about potential food sources. Characteristically, they make a determined, full-on attack. There have even been times the strikes were so violent, the rod tip was pulled into the water. Once you manage to stick one, in a fighting tactic similar to jacks and pompano, perch use their flat, semi-oval profiles to "dog" you in the current.

Barred perch range from Point Conception in California south along the Baja coast practically to the midway point of the peninsula. I'm not sure exactly why, but the best concentrations of perch seem to be in the vicinity of San Quintin which is approximately 187 miles south of the Tijuana border. The clam beds off Playa San Ramon about two miles north and the pebbly beach of Rancho Soccoro are usually loaded with perch. This is also one of my most productive halibut spots. Despite the turbulence, the water is usually clear and the sight of pillowcase halibut cruising along the shore break can cause you to forget about the perch.

The perch are not only abundant in this area, they also tend to be large. Obviously, size is relative. Judged according to the total spectrum of species available to the Baja-bound angler, barred perch fall into the junior weight division. The majority that you'll catch weigh from 3/4 to 1 1/4 pounds and seldom exceed 10 or 11 inches in length. A three-pounder is considered a real trophy. Few over four pounds have been recorded. However, what they lack in size is certainly compensated for in terms of the great sport they give you on fly gear.

Good perch fishing can be had practically on a year-round basis in Baja, but the optimum months are from January to mid-April. In preparation for spawning at the beginning of the year, the larger females move into the surf zone from deeper water. It's during this period that you have your best chance of taking prize specimens close to the three-pound mark.

While barred perch bear a resemblance to bluegill and crappie, the designation "bonefish of the beach" belongs to the corbina. Both in terms of overall body shape and fighting characteristics, corbina are not a far cry from the highly prized gray ghosts of the tropical flats. The two species feed mostly on the bottom. Once hooked, unlike perch which are characteristically short-spurt sprinters, corbina, like bonefish, tend to be long distance runners. During midsummer and early fall when corbina are most abundant, like bonefish, they are often plainly visible as they grub for food practically at the water's edge. Under conditions like this, the presentation strategy involves sight casting to cruising fish just as you would for bonefish.

Since corbina frequently cruise back and forth only a few feet from where the water rushes up on the beach, wading usually isn't necessary. Besides, in the surf, it can be dangerous. For perch, halibut, and bass, when I'm trying to reach some of those deeper pockets, I only venture out about up to my knees. However, where corbina are concerned, often times it's best to cast from a crouching position on dry sand. They may not be as wary as bonefish or permit, but corbina do

Halibut have a formidable set of dentures.

spook easily if they are aware of your presence, so try to be as unobtrusive as possible.

Even if you don't frighten them off, corbina are the most difficult of all surf zone species to entice with artificials. Like the perch and yellowfin croaker a substantial part of their diet consists of sandcrabs. However, despite your faith in the reproduction, when it isn't the real thing, the corbina's refusals will give new meaning to the term frustration. I've raised the eyebrows of more than one Florida Keys guide when I've said that I find them more difficult to take on flies than permit.

Yellowfin croaker used to be prevalent in the Southern California surf, but sadly this is no longer the case. According to health bulletins, they're not even fit to eat. Fortunately, there are still abundant populations along the Baja coastline. Locally they are sometimes referred to as tom cod, but regardless of what you call them, these croakers will readily take the same flies you cast to perch and corbina. Unlike cruising corbina, you seldom see them, but they frequent the same waters. Even when I caught them off Southern California beaches, the croaker were small, seldom going more than a pound. In Baja the specimens are larger. I've hit some yellowfin that were in the three-pound class and they make for some nice action in the surf.

Since sandcrabs are a major dietary item for perch, corbina, and croaker, I tie many of my surf patterns to simulate these oval-shaped, nickel- and dime-size crustaceans. Their presence is sometimes indicated by V-shaped indentations in the sand. If you're barefoot, sometimes you can feel them as they burrow beneath you. Another indication are sandpipers. When these graceful birds are darting back and forth along the water's edge, they're more than likely feeding on sandcrabs. If it's a sandcrab bed they're pecking at, chances are there will be fish in the vicinity trying to get their share. So, whenever you encounter sandpipers busily feeding, it's a good idea to fan out a few casts in the area.

The crabs vary in color from light tan to gray. The females that may be laden with roe carry a bright orange sack on their abdomen. When tying sandcrab type flies, it isn't necessary to strive for an exact imitation. One of the most lifelike renditions I've ever come across was a rubber artificial. Looking at it, you had a difficult time distinguishing it from the real thing. Apparently though, the fish were able to tell the difference. I never met a spin fisherman who ever caught anything on them.

Instead of exact replicas, tie your flies to simulate the basic size and color of these tiny mole crabs. Two patterns I simply call Sandcrab Dark and Sandcrab Light are good examples. (They are illustrated in Lefty Kreh's book, *Saltwater Fly Patterns*). I use them for all three species, the only difference being hook sizes. For corbina, sizes 2, 4, and 6 are all good choices. For perch and yellowfin croaker, I step up to 2s, 1s, and 1/0s. The Mustad 3407 is the hook I usually tie these on. Even though I'm using sinking lines in the surf, with the churning water, the flies don't always get down as quickly as I like. If the water is very rough, I'll use these patterns tied with 5/32 ounce lead eyes.

The body material for both flies is a thin strip of rabbit fur dyed the appropriate color. Like most of my flies, the tying procedure is relatively simple. After securing the eyes immediately behind the hookeye, lay a strip of rabbit fur atop the hook shank. This should be about 1 3/4 to 2 1/2 inches in length. Bind the strip to the shank and work the thread forward approximately 1/8 inch behind the eyes. Take the remainder of the strip, palmer it around the shank and tie it off immediately behind the eyes. This results in a nice, full collar that presents a realistic silhouette in the water. To duplicate an egg sack, wrap a few turns of orange chenille around the shank just where the bend begins.

Another pattern I use for these fish is one I call the Beach Bug. I originally tied it for barred perch and corbina, but yellowfin croaker, halibut and an occasional sargo have found it to their liking. It features green-dyed grizzly saddle hackles similar in color to the motor oil-hued plastic tails that produce so well for spin fishermen working the surf. Again, to aid the fly's sink rate, I tie in a pair of 7/32 ounce dumbbell eyes and paint them black.

Surf Zone Halibut

Admittedly, halibut are not a species that come readily to mind in fly fishing circles. They are primarily bottom dwellers. However, they just don't lie there like discarded floor mats with no apparent purpose. Instead, they're constantly on the lookout for a meal. They have an undulating skirt of fins around their body that enables them to wriggle into sandy or muddy bottoms until they are nearly covered with only their eyes exposed. However, most of the ones I've

taken on fly off the stone-studded beaches south of San Quintin, were cruising a long shore break searching for an opportunity to ambush prey. Even when lying still, halibut can intercept prey with the best of them. Their lightning-quick darts are made possible by their ability to force water through their gills. This propels their slightly elongated, frisbee-shaped torso in a jet-like thrust. In the shallow water surf, the velocity of this thrust can actually cause them to break the surface when they're chasing prey. This has happened to me several times just as I was about to lift the fly from the water in preparation for another cast.

Unlike other surf zone species, even in the fish-rich waters along Baja's coast, halibut seldom seem to congregate in schools like they do in deeper water. Given this fact, just as in the case with perch, it's important to work the fly over vast stretches of bottom.

Of all the surf-based species, halibut are about the only ones where you sometimes have to worry about getting bit off. They sport a formidable set of dentures. Nonetheless, most of the time I don't like to use a shock leader. Just like their Southern California cousins, these fish south of the border can get leader shy so I usually tie the fly directly to the class tippet. You can tangle with halibut in the 10- to 15-pound class down here and for that reason, I don't use tippets as light as the ones I tie up for the wary corbina. Heavy line can turn off both species, but with corbina I can go as light as 8- or 6-pound test. For halibut, it's best to use at least 12-pound.

More so than perch and corbina, halibut are opportunistic feeders and will dine on a host of morsels including crabs, squid, anchovies, grunion, smelt, queenfish and mackerel. During spring grunion runs in Southern California, which are publicized in local papers, try and make a trip south of the border because these prime baitfish will be engaged in similar spawning rituals along sandy Baja beaches. Halibut and calico bass love them. Both halibut and calicos also have a fondness for barred perch fry. Like grunion, the juvenile perch have bright silver coloration and this should be incorporated into your fly patterns. Deceivers and Clouser Minnow patterns from one and a half to five inches in length will get the halibut's and calico's attention.

Another pattern that I've had particularly good success with lately doesn't really have a specific name. I originally got the idea for the fly from Bob Popovics' Siliclone series, so I guess we can call it a Bend Back Siliclone. The hook I use is one of my favorites and most fly tiers I show it to quickly adopt it. It's an Owner Spinnerbait hook. The diameter is fairly small, but it's strong and the pre-sharpened point is incredibly sharp. I even use this hook for some offshore flies. The model number is 5320 and the size I like for halibut is a 1/0. For calicos and their bucket-size mouths, I frequently use 3/0s.

The first step in tying this fly is to bend the hook back slightly so it will ride in the water with the point facing up. Grasp the shank with pliers approximately 3/4 of an inch behind the hookeye. With the point facing up, press down on the hook shank. All you want to do here is make a slight bend in the shank. If the bend is too deep, you won't get positive hook sets and you'll miss a lot of strikes.

To ensure that the fly will ride upside down, I make a keel using the lead filaments that I break off from lead-core lines. Place the hook in a vise in the usual manner with the point facing down. Take an inch-and-a-half length of lead and lay it along the top side of the hook shank. Bind it down with white fly tying thread. Be sure that the lead doesn't wrap around the shank, otherwise the fly may not ride properly. Turn the hook over in the vise so that the point is now facing up. Take a medium bunch of white bucktail, about 3 1/2 inches in length, and tie it in behind the hookeye. To give the fly some flash, tie in about two dozen strands of Sparkle Flash. The green pearl color works very well and I use it on many of the flies I tie for Baja.

The head section of this fly is tied "Popovics style", and involves a combination of sheep fleece and silicone. Tie in a medium portion of white fleece about an inch long and flare it "bucktail fashion" so that it covers the top (point side) and sides of the hook. When working with wool, fleece or various synthetics such as macramé cord, a wire brush like those sold in pet stores is useful for brushing the material out, causing it to flare. Bring the thread forward and tie it off behind the hookeye. Remove the fly from the vise and trim the fleece so that you have a slightly rounded head that tapers in the front and rear. When you have the desired shape, apply a light coat of clear silicone over the entire head section. Lay a pair of 3/16-inch eyes on each side of the head. Then apply a second light coat of silicone. To get a nice, smooth finish, wet your finger with saliva or use photo flow which can be purchased at most photography stores. Gently stroke the silicone with your wetted finger always working toward the rear of the fly. If you try to work your finger back and forth, you'll ruin the finish. It takes a little practice, but when you do it right, you can get a finish that's almost as smooth as glass. Depending on the brand of silicone, drying time will vary, but generally it will take about a half hour before it begins to set. You should probably wait at least a few hours before fishing the fly.

This may seem like a lot of trouble to go through for a fly, but it really isn't. Besides, the finished product is more than worth it in terms of the effectiveness with which you will be able to fish it in the surf. For this type of fishing, you can't beat a bend back or Clouser style where the hook point rides up. Not only will the fly not hang up as readily on the bottom, but the point will stay sharper much longer. If the hook point is pulled through the sand, it will dull in no time at all.

Two other qualities that you should incorporate in all your flies that take on added significance in the surf zone, are durability and resistance to fouling. The fly may look great, but if it doesn't hold up to the ravages of the surf it isn't going to do you much good. That's the case with many of the sand-crab imitations tied with bucktail that's been pulled back over the top of the hook. The fly looks realistic enough but it doesn't last. After it's dragged across a sandbar a few times the bucktail breaks and shreds and now the "crab" looks like it's sporting a punk rock hairdo.

Alright, so now that you have your flies how should they be worked in the surf? Well, the retrieve doesn't have to be fancy. Water turbulence alone will impart considerable movement for you. As in other facets of this sport, there are no hard and fast rules to go by. You might start out with a medium-paced retrieve with some brief pauses in between. In any case, do not be afraid to alter the stripping pace. It may take some experimenting before things start to happen.

The other problem you want to avoid are flies that foul easily. In all my years of fly fishing, if there is one thing I can say for certain, it's that fish will not hit fouled flies. Particularly when casting from a beach on the Pacific side of the peninsula, more often than not you'll be throwing into the wind. This fact coupled with the churning water can readily cause trailing material like bucktail or hackle to foul around the hook bend.

Calico Bass and White Seabass

In Southern California, calicos and, particularly, white seabass, are the species that most anglers associate with fishing from a boat. Calicos are caught in the Southern California surf, whites very seldom are. Both are fairly abundant in Baja, although for fly fishermen, taking white seabass in the surf is not very common. I took a few back in the early 70s. As far as I know, they may have been the first taken on fly off the beach. You'll have much better success fishing them from a boat, and a good place for this is the other side of the peninsula in Bahia de Los Angeles.

With calicos though, a shore-based fly fisherman on Baja's Pacific side can fare quite well. Like the other surf species, you can get into calicos right after you cross the border at Tijuana. Some of the most productive spots, however, are the rocky stretches from Colonet to just slightly north of Guerrero Negro. A place where I've made some of my most memorable catches is between Santa Rosalita and Punta Rosarito. My late friend, Ron Rock, first brought me to this spot back in 1974. Sadly, he and his wife lost their lives in a car accident on Highway 1 driving down to this very spot. Ronney fished conventional gear but he used to get a kick out of watching me do my thing with the fly rod. In time, he began to consider it as a serious fishing tool. Just about every trip we made there, we caught so many different species, we eventually named the place "Variety". It's where I took my first white seabass, corvina and sargo on a fly. Yellowfin croaker are there in good numbers and so are the calicos.

Sargo tend to be a rarity, at least on fly, and the corvina here are not as plentiful as they used to be. If you want to fish for these Baja versions of sea trout, your best bet is the Rocky Point area across from Cholla Bay not far from San Felipe in the northern tip of the Sea of Cortez. For more information on this interesting fishery contact the personnel at the Arizona Fly Fishing Store in Tempe. Their number is (602) 730-6808.

Both calicos and white seabass favor rocky structure. Reefs, partially exposed boulders, rocky points, ledges and drop-offs are where you want to fish for bass. The structure

Calico bass, a prolific inshore species along Baja's coast.

Aside from the absence of sea grass, the ideal water conditions for the surf are times when it is neither too calm nor unbearably rough. A flat, calm, glassy smooth surface may be fine for spot casting to corbina, but it isn't ideal for most of the other species.

The Bend Back, Deceivers, and Clousers all work fine for bass, both calicos and whites. To realize their potential however, they have to be worked in the fish's feeding zones. We're talking structure here. Make your casts as close as possible to rocks and ledges. If you've never done this before, you'll be amazed at how effectively you can fish these areas with fly tackle. Even with fast sinking lines, the fly doesn't quickly plummet below the surface, so you can avoid hanging up on the rocks a lot easier than lure fishermen. If you carry a few different density fly lines with you, (with shooting heads this is easy to do) matching the conditions at hand becomes a simple matter of changing lines. If the water is less than 10 feet deep and there isn't too much turbulence, you might try one of the slower sinking lines. On the other hand, if it's deep and a strong current is running, get out the lead-core.

Not only are calicos fairly decent size fish in the 3- to 6-pound class, they also tend to be considerably stronger than the ones typically caught in kelp beds from boats. The reason for this is simple. They're in better shape. Living and feeding in the surf is a tough existence and these fish behave accordingly.

Lure fishermen using plastic tails often describe the calico's strike as subtle. For some reason, it's not like that with flies. Often the fly will be taken as it sinks so you should be alert for this. But even in these circumstances, with the line in your hands, the sensation is immediately telegraphed. This is an additional advantage of fly tackle in this type of environment. Because the line is retrieved manually, the fly fisherman can react instantly. With structure-loving fish like calicos, the quicker you can get the fish coming your way, the better your chance of landing it. In a situation like this, don't even think about trying to get the fish on the reel. Instead, play it by applying pressure and recovering line manually. In many cases, it's no exaggeration to liken this to a tug-of-war contest.

Obviously, when playing a fish in the surf, you have to contend with it and the elements as well. White seabass in this area routinely top the 20-pound mark. If you're lucky enough to connect with one, there are a few things you should know about landing good size fish in the surf. A fish like this could be one of those significant catches that you'll remember for a lifetime. Naturally, you will be excited. However, don't become overeager and try to muscle the fish onto the beach. With halibut, you have to be especially careful. Even though they have needle-sharp teeth and powerful jaws, the fleshy part of a halibut's mouth is soft. If you put too much pressure on the fish, the hook can easily pull out.

The simple but effective strategy is to have the waves do some of the work for you. When you have the fish fairly close to the beach and the water begins receding, resist the temptation to pull back. The added strain can easily pop the tippet. Water rushing seaward can amount to a significant force and

provides a haven for bait and it also serves as ambush cover for larger predators.

Spring and summer can be very good for bass, but regardless of what time of year it is, be advised that beach fishing for calicos is not for sleepy heads. If you must have your breakfast, put it off until later, like around 8:00 a.m. By then, the calico bite is usually over. Calicos apparently are very light sensitive, so after the sun first hits the horizon, you can plan on having about an hour or so of prime fishing time. If the weather is overcast, and it frequently is on Baja's Pacific side, the peak fishing period will be extended a little longer.

It also helps to have the right water conditions. Unfortunately, up-to-the-minute local weather reports are difficult to come by for this part of Baja. When you drive down you take your chances. There have been a number of times when friends and I were really disappointed because the surf was choked with sea grass. The fish may have been there, but you couldn't get to them. If this happens when you're at Santa Rosalillito and you have the time, head over to the Bay of L.A. It's not that long a drive, and you'll have a lot better fishing.

Jeff Solis and a Baja bonefish.

you don't want to do anything that will magnify it. If anything, it's best to run to the water's edge or push the rod forward to decrease the strain. Then, when the water starts to push forward again, apply pressure and literally try and surf the fish in.

The optimum tackle class for perch, corbina and croaker in the surf are 8- and 9-weight outfits with sinking shooting heads. When it is very calm and there is little wind, you could go as light as 6-weights, but I certainly would not rely on these as my primary outfits. The 8- and 9-weights will also work for calico bass and halibut, but since these fish are larger and more powerful than the aforementioned species, many times you will find it more practical to go with larger outfits like 10-weights. Especially considering the "bad neighborhoods" that surf calicos typically frequent, the added backbone of the heavier rod is needed to wrench them out of the structure. If you have your sights set on a white seabass, definitely use the 10-weight.

Bonefish in Baja

No, you are not misreading the title of this section. When I tell fly fishermen there are bonefish to be had in Baja, the typical response is something like, "you have to be kidding." For years, my reaction was basically the same. I was told similar tales about bonefish supposedly in the back bay of Newport Beach and didn't give that much credence either. However, my skepticism changed when I received news from a reliable source with the California Department of Fish and Game, to the effect that bonefish have indeed been caught in Newport

Bay. Then I started to reconsider the reports of bonefish in Baja. The late Tom Miller, who knew Baja about as well as anyone, mentioned bonefish in his book, *The Angler's Guide to Baja California*. However, he made only passing reference to them stating that they could be found in shallow estuaries from Laguna Manuela to above La Paz.

Laguna Manuela is close to the surf fishing spot I referred to as "Variety". It's about an hour's drive south of Punta Prieta, west of the little town, Villa Jesus Maria. There's a dirt road into the lagoon that's usually in fairly good condition, so you can generally make it in without a 4-wheel-drive vehicle. I had fished this area for years, but never thought about the prospect of bonefish. Fishing for pinto bass (a close relative of the calico) in the inlets was so good that I never had the inclination to wade the tidal flats. After meeting Jeff Solis, I realized this was a big mistake on my part. Jeff, who owns the Fly Shop in San Diego, was the first to show me photographs of bonefish he caught on these flats. I was so inspired by this that on one of my trips to the east cape, I canceled the return flight and elected to drive back home with my friend Gary Graham on the condition that we stop at Manuela Laguna and give the bones a try. We were on a tight schedule and could manage only an hour's fishing time. We didn't catch any bonefish that first time out, but the trip was worth all the effort because I saw my first Baja bonefish. The tide was dead low and I spooked a fish that I didn't expect to be so close to me.

To fish this area properly, you should try and hit the tide about an hour before it is high. Bonefish will start coming close in to shore to feed. That is when you'll experience some of the most consistent action. The timing won't be up-to-the-minute, but you can get a good approximation of the tidal changes by consulting a tide book for the San Diego area.

With the exception of a few local differences, the tackle and technique are pretty much the same as would apply to more familiar bonefish environments. Because these flats are close to the open ocean, the wind can get strong, so I seldom fish anything lighter than an 8-weight outfit. The water depth varies from ankle- to shin-deep, so an intermediate line is definitely appropriate. You could use a floater here, but with the gentle wave action, an intermediate line will track straighter. This gives you a better feel for the fly's movement in the water so even subtle strikes are more readily detected. This is also the kind of fishing where you want to use longer leaders. A nine-foot leader is about right, and if you are not sure of the length, use your fly rod as a guide.

The flies to use here are standard bonefish patterns. Tan Clouser Minnows tied on number 4 hooks seem to work particularly well. As a general rule of thumb, try and select a color pattern that blends in with the bottom. If you have a fly that is in stark contrast to its surroundings, particularly the bottom, it will appear unnatural. Nature did not design prey to be easily recognizable. An organism that stood out and made for an easy target would have been eaten to the point of early extinction. Food sources like small crabs that match the color of the sand do get eaten, but the fish have to hunt for them. They'll do the same with your flies.

R. V. DUIJNHOVEN

Protective footwear and a stripping basket are important auxiliary items for fly fishing the surf.

One aspect of this fishery that differs somewhat from more traditional bonefishing, is the placement of your casts. Because there are a series of wavelets that wash over the flat, the bonefish are often not plainly visible. By all means, cast to fish you have spotted. However, for those times when nothing appears visible, cast anyway because there may be fish in the area that you cannot see.

As in any bonefishing area, the fish are not always congregated on the tidal flats, but when they are, they will usually take flies readily. At one to three pounds, these fish are in the junior weight division but they are still fun to catch on fly gear and it's a great way to round out a surf fishing trip.

Auxiliary Gear for the Surf

As we stated at the beginning of this chapter, for fly fishermen, the surf can be a pretty intimidating place. However, with the right auxiliary gear, you'll find that most of the time you can fish here comfortably and effectively. Let's talk comfort first.

To the surprise of many, the Pacific Ocean, even down Baja way, is cold. The water temperature here is frequently only in the 60s. Many of the surfers wear neoprene wet suits all year long. True, they're totally immersed in the water, something you want to avoid. Nevertheless, a pair of chest high waders, preferably neoprene, will keep you warm and dry. I like the boot-foot type simply because they are easy to put on and take off. During the summer months the water does warm up a bit so you might get by with just a pair of shorts.

However, even under these circumstances, some type of protective footwear is recommended. In places the sand can be very coarse. Some beaches consist of broken pieces of clam shells and walking on them barefoot would be pure torture. Jagged rocks pose the same problem. In addition, if I see a spot I want to get to quickly, I want to be able to run there without worrying about what I might be stepping on. A bad cut on your foot or some other similar mishap can ruin a trip in short order. Despite the availability of clinics in some areas, Baja is no place you want to get injured.

For those times you do wade wet, a pair of neoprene diving booties is a good choice. If you can find the slip-on kind with no zippers, so much the better. When they become choked with sand, zippers can be harder to move than a stubborn mule. One way of preventing this is to wear a pair of gravel guards. Get the kind with Velcro fasteners. These wrap around your ankles, and in addition to keeping the sand out, they provide added protection for your ankles in rocky areas.

To fish the surf effectively, one item that you should never be without is a stripping basket. Some people are turned off by them right from the start. That's usually because they haven't really spent any time with them. It doesn't take long to become familiar with one to the point where wearing a basket is as natural as donning a fly fishing vest. Most places in the surf I wouldn't even bother fly fishing without one. That's how important I regard them.

You can buy them or make them yourself. Mesh-type baskets offer the convenience of easy portability. However, when luggage space is not a concern, I opt for a rigid basket.

Especially if you are using a mono running line, go with a deep basket. The best I've found is a rubber wastepaper container. It's 15 inches deep and 7 inches wide. The flat sides align nicely against your hip and the depth prevents the line from easily spilling out. Since wading out in the surf over your knees is not a good idea anyway, the basket can be worn waist-high without restricting any movement. Using a heated nail, I punch holes in the bottom so water will quickly drain out. Two holes are also punched in the side so I can run a bungee cord through it as a belt.

If you are planning to wade waist deep, I recommend switching to a basket with more shallow dimensions. A rubber dish pan is ideal. This type is worn waist-high in front of you. With the basket in this position, a two-handed stripping technique is best. The line will fall directly into the basket.

Finally, no matter where you are fly fishing, always make it a practice to wear eyeglasses regardless of the condition of your vision. Polarized lenses are great even in the surf because they help you identify many of the fish-holding features discussed.

Chapter IV

Shoreline Species on Baja's East Coast

Variety is not only an appropriate description for Baja's species, it also characterizes the different locales from which to fish. Perhaps the most dramatic example of this is the contrasting environments on the east and west sides of the peninsula. The Pacific side is a classic surf setting. There are some quiet spots in several of the large lagoons like Laguna Manuela, but these represent mere interludes in an otherwise turbulent setting. Instead, high rolling waves, crashing breakers and churning water are the hallmarks of the Pacific shore which prevail all the way down the coast to the tip of the peninsula.

Once you round the Cape, however, and begin working your way north along the eastern shore, the conditions seem like a world apart. Compared to the Pacific, the water along the eastern shore can be as tranquil as a Midwest farm pond. It's a subtropical setting where the sea almost seems to lick the shore rather than pound it. At times the wind can create a nasty chop, but the effect isn't too different from what you might encounter on a large, inland lake. All in all, the Sea of Cortez side of the peninsula is considerably more hospitable to the shore-bound fly fisherman. Currently there are two angling services that specialize in fly fishing this region. In Cabo, there is Baja Anglers (888-894-FISH) and at the East Cape, Baja on the Fly (800-919-BAJA).

Ladyfish, "the poor man's tarpon".

Baitfish fleeing for their lives.

With the exception of a turbulent surf, the Baja coastline, particularly from La Paz south to Cabo San Lucas (the famed East Cape) offers basically the same type of beach terrain that is found on the Pacific side. There are rock outcroppings, coves, long stretches of sandy beach, shoreline drop-offs and inshore reefs. The fishing can be excellent in all these locales, however, the key to consistent success is timing.

As is true in any shoreline fishing, the tides certainly have an influence on the movement and availability of bait which, in turn, attracts larger predators. But on the Sea of Cortez side of the peninsula, a more important variable seems to be the time of day rather than the tidal phase. If you spend any time fishing the beach down here, you will find that the best action typically occurs during those periods when the light intensity is minimal. These are the time periods I like to refer to as the "grays". Early morning before the sun has hit the horizon can be a magical time for the beach-based fly fisherman. Baitfish tend to move close in to shore and their pursuers are never far behind.

What is so exciting about this time period is that often you can see the drama between predator and prey played out right before your eyes and only a few yards from where you're standing. In these early-morning feeding sprees, baitfish are sometimes pushed right up on the beach. Whether they make it to the beach or not, their fate is sealed. They may have escaped the pursuing game fish only to become easy meals for swooping seabirds that scoop up their targets with unrelenting accuracy. Present a fly in the midst of a scene like this and it will rarely be refused.

In the event you have taken the trouble to rise this early and see no signs of life, do not despair and do not stand idly by waiting for something to happen. Cast your fly. Baitfish and their pursuers don't always make their presence known by virtue of surface disturbances on the water. The two could be playing out their survival script an easy cast away, but the light is low and you can't see them in the water. Better yet, they can't see you either. Under these conditions, game fish lose some of their natural wariness and they are more likely to strike something, even if it doesn't look quite the same as what they have been feeding on.

Gary Graham knows the rewards of early-morning blind casting firsthand. Literally right in front of his house, only a half-mile or so south of Rancho Buena Vista, he took a jack crevalle that made the record books. Along the same stretch of beach we have taken roosters, ladyfish and pompano casting during early-morning periods when the sea seemed lifeless.

Though the action usually is not as fast paced, late afternoon and dusk are also good times to fly fish these beaches. Again, it's the low light conditions that bring in the baitfish and trigger the feeding rituals of the predators. There can also be an added bonus to the afternoon period that surprisingly few anglers are aware of. The fishing boats from the lodges begin dispatching their fishermen-clients in the late afternoon and during the process they dump bait that may still be in the live wells. Jacks and roosterfish seem to be attuned to this ritual because they'll come to within casting range of the shore to dine on the leftovers. Hitting the pool, having a few drinks or just relaxing in one of the hotel rooms is a great way to kick back after a long day out on the water, but if you forego these pleasures a while longer and start casting the beach, often you

The Sea of Cortez side of Baja peninsula is an ideal setting for shore-bound fly fishermen.

Early morning is a prime time for inshore action.

a good chance of hooking up with a junior version of the wahoo in the form of sierra mackerel.

For many people, spring is a very welcome season. It's a time of reawakening in the outdoors and a respite from the harshness of winter. It's also a good time to fish in Baja, especially for those who like to remain inshore. Springtime is regarded as part of the off season and booking hotels and lodges is generally no problem. In addition, the weather is typically more comfortable compared to the soaring summertime temperatures that climb well into the nineties. Windy conditions are the one downside to this time of year and can put a damper on offshore fishing.

However, for shore-side fishermen, the wind can be a blessing in disguise. The wind can turn the normally gin-clear water murky and this works to the advantage of anglers fishing from the beach. Similar to what you find in low light conditions, baitfish congregate close to shore when water clarity diminishes. Maybe they're trying to take refuge in the cloudy water. Whatever the reason, it isn't a good move because larger fish always seem to find them.

For fly fishermen a most welcome predator is the sierra. Pound for pound they are probably the fastest, most aggressive inshore game fish that you'll encounter in Baja.

Low light conditions at sunset can yield a variety of species.

can be rewarded with some fine catches. True, it doesn't happen often, but there are times when anglers working the beach catch more fish than they did out in the boats.

Practically all the species available to the East Cape, shore-based angler are also caught from the boats. There is no argument that in terms of pure fishing efficiency, boats are the best bet. You can cover more water quickly and get into fish that beach casters could never hope to reach. However, this book is about fly fishing, so right from the start we've ruled out considerations of peak efficiency. Besides, fishing the beach has a charm all its own that can never be duplicated by standing on the deck of a boat. Most of the species I'm about to discuss, I have caught from both the shore and from boats, and I've always found the former experiences to be far more significant.

Because of the overlap between beach and boat fishing, in this next section I will confine myself to a few major species that are readily available to shore-bound fly fishermen. There are striped mullet, goat fish, a variety of grunts and exotics like cornetfish and gafftopsail pompano that will all take flies. Conditions permitting, on 6- and 7-weight outfits they're fun to catch, but they are not considered significant game fish species. The other species that will be omitted from this section is the roosterfish. A limited number of roosters have been taken off the beach on fly. However, it is such a prized species that it merits its own separate section.

Sierra, Ladyfish and Needlefish

Few fly fishermen have had the opportunity to do battle with wahoo. They typically require fairly extensive offshore outings and even then, they are not easy to come by. There is a smaller scale alternative however. If you can arrange to be at the East Cape from about December to early spring, you stand

A beautiful example of the pompano family.

Characterizing them as mini wahoo is not an exaggeration, but it's certainly an excellent set of credentials as far as game fish are concerned.

Sierra are a lot of fun to catch from boats. They are an absolute blast to tangle with off the beach. There's no doubt when they strike your fly. The take transfers to your line hand more like a jolt, as if something were trying to rip the fly from its intended path. When you get hit, don't try and look for the fish. Instead, focus on the remaining loose line. It's going to shoot up out of the stripping basket like a tightly coiled steel spring that's suddenly unloading. After it clears, be prepared for line stripping bursts that will make your reel's drag scream. If you're fortunate enough to slide one of these sleek beauties up on the beach, be very careful when removing the fly because sierra have a nasty set of dentures. You might luck out without it, but this is one inshore species where you should be using wire. To enable the fly to turn over properly, use a short, four- to five-inch section of 27-pound test, single strand, dark colored wire.

The sierra's favorite food sources are anchovies and sardinas, so your flies should resemble these baitfish. My Sardina pattern, small Deceivers two to four inches long, Clouser Minnows and Popovics' 3-D Fly all work fine for sierra. The best single color is white with flash material tied in like Flashabou or Sparkle Flash. Blue and white and green and white combinations are also good color choices. Like wahoo, sierra are high speed predators. They generally prefer to run down their prey so a fast-paced, steady retrieve usually draws the most strikes.

In the introduction to this section we talked about the effectiveness of blind casting. Casting when there are no apparent signs can produce strikes from sierra, but more often than not this is one fish that usually announces its presence with highly visible surface splashes and considerable bird activity. In this respect, sierra on the feed are very much like the bluefish blitzes off the East Coast back in the states. For those times when you don't see any signs, try working

points, coves and drop offs. They are favorite feeding areas for sierra.

Another excellent inshore fighter is the ladyfish. In Spanish it is known as sabalo and machete. In Central America and the Yucatan, tarpon are referred to as sabalo and, though they are a different species, the ladyfish is often called "the poor man's tarpon".

This is an exciting little game fish. It seldom tips the scales at more than three pounds, but it will offer great sport on an 8-weight outfit. The sierra may be the fastest inshore species, but the ladyfish is the acrobatic queen. Its high flying leaps and uncanny ability to rid itself of hooks are two characteristics it shares in common with tarpon.

The same flies you cast to sierra will also work for ladyfish. The important consideration here is to try and match the size of the baitfish the ladyfish are feeding on. Obviously, if they are ambushing two-inch-long sardinas, flies that are four inches long will not draw many strikes. In addition, if you want to target ladyfish, do not use wire leaders. Ladyfish do not have cutting teeth like sierra and they tend to be much

A roosterfish off the beach.

JEFF SOLIS

A small jack taken blind casting.

more leader conscious. Tie the fly directly to an 8- or 12-pound test class tippet and you'll have a lot more action. However, be sure to check the tippet after every encounter with a ladyfish (this is good practice for any species) because their dental structure is very abrasive on mono. Like the sierra, ladyfish are programmed for high speed pursuit, so fast retrieves seem to work best. When you feel the strike, continue to strip until the fish actually begins to take out line. Ladyfish are very adept at throwing the fly.

Blind casting is also highly recommended for this species. Even though ladyfish can cause a great deal of surface commotion when they're chasing bait, there are many times when their presence is not indicated by any visible signs. Occasionally you can see them swimming parallel to the beach in fairly large schools, but when they're moving like this, it's very difficult to get them to strike. The same is true for small jack crevalle. For some reason, when these fish are travelling close to the beach in tightly packed schools, they are not interested in feeding.

Casting even when there are no apparent signs of fish in the area can pay dividends, particularly with ladyfish. Of course, you don't want to cast haphazardly. Ladyfish seem to prefer sandy bottoms, but unlike bonefish, they'll seldom congregate over shallow, open areas. Instead, like most other inshore predators, they prefer to do their hunting along drop-offs, cuts and ridges that parallel the shore. On the Sea of Cortez side, there isn't much in the way of wave patterns to help you read the bottom. So what you should look for are abrupt changes in water color. The water will tend to be a darker shade over deep slots in the bottom and this is where you want to concentrate your casts.

The one species you can spend a lot of time sight casting to is the needlefish. They share two characteristics in common with sierra. They have a wicked set of teeth and they seem to travel just about everywhere in pursuit of baitfish. Sandy bot-

toms, reefs, rock outcroppings; you'll find needlefish in all kinds of habitat as long as there are baitfish present.

In terms of sheer length, if not in pounds, the needlefish is one of the largest inshore predators that you'll encounter off the beach in Baja. I have hooked a number of fish in the 5-foot range and there are specimens that have measured close to 6 feet.

Notice I used the word hooked. Needlefish will readily take flies. Just about anything with a sleek, baitfish silhouette and a lot of flash will get their attention. Burn the fly through the water and they'll tear after it. They will also tear up your flies. And if you don't use wire leaders, plan on donating a lot of flies.

Inducing them to strike isn't too difficult, but getting the hook to remain in place is a whole different matter. Needlefish have a tough, elongated jaw that is studded with needle-like teeth. Couple this with the fact that they can jump like crazy when hooked and you begin to understand why such a small percentage of these fish are actually landed.

However, there is one tactic that can help tip the balance in your favor. One day a local fisherman was watching me tie flies with macramé material that I was teasing out with a wire brush. Drawing on his experience with billfish, he suggested that I make a long tail trailing behind the hook with this material. The needlefish's teeth would become embedded in the material and they wouldn't be able to dislodge the fly so

An early morning sierra mackerel.

easily. I've only done this twice with a 50 percent success rate, which is far higher than all my previous encounters with this toothy adversary.

The Midriff

One look at a map and it's easy to see how these islands got their collective name. They lie approximately halfway up the Sea of Cortez and midway between the Baja peninsula and Mexico's mainland. Down here, you know you're away from civilization. For the most part, these islands are uninhabited and seldom see many visitors save for sea birds. There are lizards and rattlesnakes on the islands. The rattlers feed on the lizards. I don't know what the lizards eat. There are some coyotes around but they're mainly nocturnal so you don't see much of them. The barren rock and volcanic terrain doesn't provide much bedding for vegetation so about the only green you see is in the form of ocean hues.

Dating back to the early Spanish explorers, these islands and channels have some colorful names that tell you something about the region. Though I haven't seen many in the area, the largest island of the group is Tiburon (shark) Island on the eastern side of the Midriff. The narrow passage between Tiburon Island and the mainland is Canal de Inferiernillo. The literal translation is "little hell". On a deep draft boat, if you navigate incorrectly, the place could turn into a big hell. One sailing manual states that the north end of the channel has many shoals and should be avoided.

Aside from shoals, this entire region can be home to some of the most dangerous water in the Sea of Cortez. Tidal flows in the Gulf of California can be quite strong, but they generally do not compare to the currents generated when the sea is compressed into the narrow confines of the Midriff. Notwithstanding the danger this can present to boaters, there is a blessing in all this. These exceptionally strong currents cause great upwellings of nutrient-rich water from the depths. That's why the hues in this area are generally green instead of cobalt blue. This nitrogen-laden water sets off an ecological feeding chain that culminates with a stellar lineup of game fish. We'll get to that later.

The second largest island in the Sea of Cortez is Isla de la Guardia (guardian angel island). Maybe it got its name from some of the early sailors who survived the passage at Tiburon. To the north of this island is one of the safest anchorages in the area, Bahia Refugio (refuge bay). South of Isla Guardia you'll run into (not literally, I hope) Isla Partida and Isla Raza. The latter island is designated a national park and you should obtain permission from the government if you want to go on it. It's a breeding ground for a variety of sea birds. Continuing south there's a narrow chain of three islands: Isla Salsipuedes (get out if you can), Isla Las Animas (island of spirits), and San Lorenzo. Isla Salsipuedes may have been named for the fact that the current can be so powerful that some boats have difficulty making headway! While we're on the subject of names, I'd like to point out that the series of submerged ridges that connects this strip of islands from Isla Partida to San Lorenzo has been dubbed "yellowtail

One ladyfish that didn't throw the fly.

alley". Cabrilla and white seabass also frequent this same neighborhood.

As remote as these islands are, getting to them is not all that difficult. One option that goes almost unnoticed by fly fishermen is to charter a trip on one of the "live aboard" yachts berthed in San Felipe. Tony Reyes, one of the most likeable guys you'll ever meet, pioneered this type of fishing in the Midriff over 40 years ago. You sleep and take your meals on a large, comfortable mother ship. The rest of the time is spent fishing the Midriff from skiffs (pangas) that have been stowed aboard the mother ship. The guides are all very experienced. Because of all the years they've logged on these trips, they know the area better than anyone. Some of my best fly fishing experiences in the Gulf have been on Tony's charters. To get more information, contact the Longfin tackle store. They're located at 133 S. Yorba, Orange, CA. 92669. Tel: (714) 538-9300. Just bring plenty of flies.

Another way to go is to drive down. (We'll have more to say about driving in Baja in a separate section). Your final destination to reach this area is Bahia de Los Angeles, better known as L.A. Bay. It lies roughly 400 miles south of Tijuana. Driving safely, that translates into about 9 1/2 to 11 hours travelling time.

The city itself lies at the base of a 5,000-foot mountain. It doesn't have the glitz and glamour of a place like Cabo San Lucas, and for many, that's what makes the place so charming. It's like travelling back in time a century or more when life unfolded at a more relaxed pace. Of course, what goes along with this simplified existence is a lack of many of the amenities we have come to take for granted.

Like practically all of Baja, but especially here, if you're driving down, be totally self contained. That means having the basics like water and gas. Sammy Dias, of the Dias family who have been here for ages, has a little store where ice is usually available. There's a gas station across the street, but getting fuel can be a chancy proposition. The Villa Vitta, Guillermos

When conditions are right, white seabass will readily take flies.

Harry Kime, at Loreto, with yellowtail.

and Las Hamacas all offer lodging, some excellent meals and RV parks. The parks are little more than places where you can park your rig. A few miles north of town, there's the Ejido Trailer Park. In the other direction, a few miles south, you'll find Gecco Park which is very rustic (small rooms with palm roofs). There are a number of launch ramps but the one at Villa Vitta is best.

Almost anyone in town can help find you a guide. Even if you have your own boat, if you are unfamiliar with the area, I strongly recommend a guide. Not only are you likely to get into a lot more fish, more importantly, you will do so more safely. The winds down here can suddenly appear almost out of nowhere and turn an otherwise calm surface into a very turbulent sea. There are at least 15 tiny islands where you can run to get out of the weather, but it helps to know exactly where you're going.

In addition to the aforementioned islands, some of the better known spots in the area are Isla Coronado (a.k.a Smith Island). The northeast side of this island can be particularly good for yellowtail. Isla Piojo and Punta Don Juan feature good yellowtail and cabrilla fishing. At Isla Pata, and Punta La Gringa in the spring, you can encounter white seabass and halibut. In summer, Punta Quemalo can be a hot spot for dorado while an occasional sail can be had off Punta Roja. The problem here is that there are so many good places holding so many different varieties of fish, that sometimes it's difficult to choose a spot.

White Seabass and Yellowtail

We briefly mentioned white seabass in the previous chapter. However, I want to say more about them in this section because the chances of scoring on them with fly tackle are much better on this side of the peninsula.

Rating game fish is highly subjective. Often it simply boils down to a case of "different strokes for different folks". Be that as it may, the general consensus is that the most highly coveted game fish in the northern part of the Sea of Cortez is the white seabass. This overgrown member of the croaker family is highly prized for a number of reasons.

First, and I don't mean to offend those who are strictly into catch and release, white seabass are some of the finest eating fish to ever grace a table. Unfortunately, that fact has had a severe impact on their stocks both in Southern California and Baja. They do seem to be on the comeback though, and hopefully this trend will continue.

Secondly, the white seabass is an inshore species that grows relatively large and is receptive to a large variety of offerings. In terms of size, in my bait fishing days, I took whites over 60 pounds in the surf on dead squid. Fish in the 20- and 30-pound range are not uncommon. Fortunately, for fly fishermen, if you can get on a school when the dinner bell has rung, they will eat flies. Very little is written about this because only a handful of fly fishermen have ever made the effort or had the opportunity to fish for them.

Prime areas near the Midriff are places like San Luis Gonzaga, Bahia de Los Angeles, and San Francisquito. The best time to go is during the spring months when the whites suspend over gravel bars often in water less than 30 feet deep.

As with a number of other species in the area, the white's favorite dish is squid. Obviously then, squid patterns, or at least flies that look something like squid, are what you want to be throwing. Again, I want to stress the point that you don't need exact imitations. None of these fish are programmed to count tentacles. When they are hungry, they are not too discriminating. In fact, over the years, practically all the seabass I've taken on flies have been on large Deceivers, four to six inches long. One of the most productive artificials for white seabass is a plain, white, candy bar-shaped, metal jig. Aside from a spinning or a jigging motion, there's not a whole lot of action that you get out of a chunk of metal. Nonetheless,

white seabass, and yellowtail as well, pounce on them with a vengeance. Think how they'll go for flies.

The key lies in getting the offering to the fish and this is where the conventional fishermen have a distinct advantage. Even the metal jigs designated as "light iron", sink much more quickly than most fly lines. Couple this with the fact that you will almost never see white seabass breezing just below the surface. They simply don't do it. So, if you want to stand a decent chance of taking one on fly, you have to get it down into their feeding zone. That is why your best shot is in spring when these fish are in fairly shallow water.

White seabass have a dental structure that feels abrasive to the touch, but bait fishermen routinely catch them on 20-pound test line without experiencing many break-offs. I've caught them with and without shock leaders. If you do use one, 40-pound test will be sufficient. The ones that are broken off, are usually done so on rocks. While not as strong as yellowtail, these fish can pull. An 11- or 12-weight rod with a 20-pound test class tippet is light by conventional tackle standards. With whites over the 20-pound mark you will have your hands full.

It may seem like sort of a paradox. Yellowtail are much more abundant than white seabass. You find them practically everywhere in Baja. The entire Pacific Coast and down into the Sea of Cortez, all the way to La Paz, have large populations of this muscle-bound member of the jack family. For that reason alone, compared to white seabass, anglers manage to hook far greater numbers of yellowtail. But if there were a hooked to landed ratio, the loss column would be much higher where yellowtail are concerned. Hands down, on a pound for pound basis, they are the hardest pulling inshore fish in Baja. Though nowhere near as plentiful, when it comes to a slug fest, their close cousins the amberjack are right up there with them. Grouper and pargo are also very bad critters. They pull hard, but they aren't capable of the line scorching runs that yellows make. Besides, they are seldom targeted by fly fishermen.

It was Harry Kime who first told me to expect to be humbled by yellowtail. I knew what he was talking about because I had many years of experience doing battle with yellows on

The appropriately named needlefish.

conventional gear. In fact, I couldn't believe that Harry managed to land the yellows he did on fly tackle. Like calico bass, yellowtail are a structure-loving species. They are found in many of the same "bad neighborhoods". The only problem is that yellowtail are much larger and stronger than calicos.

All of this is compounded in Baja, because the yellows tend to run considerably larger than the ones you find in Southern California. In the Sea of Cortez, 20-pound-plus fish are typical, 40-pounders are not uncommon. With conventional gear, 50-pound test is considered standard. Those who want to try and shift the odds in their favor will fish 60-pound. Even with this kind of tackle, if you manage to land 50 percent of the yellows you hook, you're considered lucky. I am not trying to dramatize the situation, this is the way it is with these fish.

Not only are Baja yellows larger, they also tend to suspend deeper, so in many cases they are simply out of practical range for fly fishermen. On occasion, I have used 45-foot lead-core lines that were on the order of telephone cable. For me, when I have to fish lines this heavy to get down, fly fishing begins to lose its appeal. Adding to the frustration, even those times when I managed to get hooked up, I lost probably close to 90 percent of the fish and that was with 12- and 13-weight rods with 20-pound class tippets.

There are few fish that can use structure to their advantage like yellowtail can. If there is one lone rock in the area, they'll try and reach it and cut you off. Many times when you hook them in deep water, they just remain suspended. Because you're fishing rock-strewn areas, they are already where they want to be and don't have to run very far. But trying to move them is another matter. When I land even a smaller yellow in the 10- to 15-pound class under these circumstances, I feel like I've really accomplished something.

It was one of these juvenile yellowtail that brought me my closest encounter with a grouper. It was at Isla Coronado. I was in a skiff about to land what I guessed to be about a five-pound yellow, when a large broomtail grouper came up and ate the yellow. End of that story.

In chapter I, I stated that practically all of the inshore fishing in Baja could be handled on 8- to 10-weight rods.

Yellowtail are the exception. In Southern California, the junior members of the family in the five- to 10-pound class are nicknamed "firecrackers". That tells you something about their fighting ability. Given the nasty habitat you have to battle them in, even with these smaller yellows, a 10-weight outfit is about the lightest I recommend. Even if they are hooked close to the surface, yellowtail inevitably dive for structure and you have to literally wrench them from the depths. It takes a rod with backbone to do this. If you are setting your sights on fish over 25 pounds, a 12- or 13-weight is what you should be using.

Because yellowtail frequent areas laden with structure, you can often go fishing for them in the absence of any surface signs like bait or birds that normally indicate that fish are in the area. Of course, this is when it pays to have the services of a local guide who knows the area. It can save you a great deal of wasted effort. Another way of finding yellows when there is no visible surface activity is to have a non-fly-fishing companion accompany you in the skiff. Because bait can be difficult to come by in Baja, a great deal of fishing is done with artificials. Particularly where yellowtail are concerned, this takes the form of jig fishing with conventional outfits. Long casts aren't usually necessary. Instead, the object is to get the jig down to where the yellows may be suspended. Sometimes this involves little more than dropping the jig over the side of the boat. Once the jig has settled into the depths, it is cranked back up often with as rapid a retrieve as possible. This mode of conventional fishing is sometimes referred to as "pumping iron", and believe me, it can be a lot of work. After about a half hour of doing this, your arms begin to feel like they have lead weights attached to them. Nevertheless, the hardcore yellowtail fishermen do this on a regular basis because it produces fish. When I have a friend with me who is jig fishing, I let him find the fish. I don't start using the fly rod until after he gets hooked up. Then I know there are yellows in the area and I can begin to do my thing.

Like the jig fishermen, when fly fishing for yellowtail that are suspended in the depths, the concern is not with making long casts. Instead, the objective is to get the fly down. This is where you want to use the fastest sinking line you have. Lead-

Bulky flies that resemble squid can be very effective for white seabass and yellowtail.

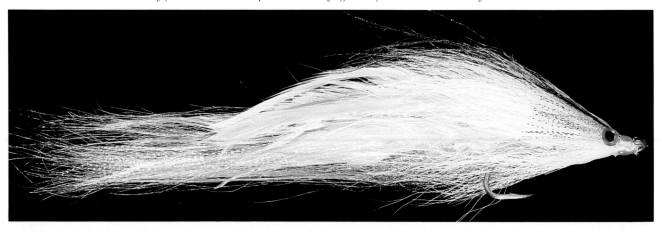

A pargo is a rare catch off the beach.

dorado, yellowfin tuna and sailfish. December through March are prime yellowtail months. The best action on cabrilla is generally March through May. Rooster fishing can be good from June all the way into November. Venturing offshore during these months can put you into dorado, yellowfin tuna and sails.

Loreto is Baja's oldest settlement. It was the region's capital from 1697 to 1827. It lies approximately 680 miles south of the border and has all the amenities for the travelling angler. There are four major hotels. La Pinta is on the beach a couple of miles north of the town plaza, La Mission is a colonial style hotel a quarter mile east of the town plaza, the Oasis is a half mile south of the plaza, and the Stouffer Presidente is on the beach about six miles south of town. There are also trailer parks, restaurants, supermarkets, banks, numerous shops and a hospital. Most convenient of all, Loreto has a major airport with daily scheduled flights.

Cabrilla and Pargo

As I stated in my first fly fishing book, *The Orvis Guide to Saltwater Fly Fishing*, cabrilla and pargo are distinct species, but I discuss them jointly because they share so much in common. Their body configuration, feeding and fighting habits, and habitat preferences are very similar.

The best action I've had fly fishing cabrilla has been on the Tony Reyes trips. The guides know all the hot spots and this will save you a lot of casting practice. On one of my first trips when I told the guide I wanted to go after cabrilla on fly, he smiled and nodded his head. I don't know if this meant that it would be no problem putting me into fish, or if it was his way

The striped pargo is a difficult fish to land on fly tackle.

core is usually my first choice here. I also like to use mono running lines, because they sink easily behind the head. Mono can be troublesome because it tangles readily and can get easily blown about by the wind. One way of reducing these problems is to use fairly heavy mono for the running line. I don't recommend anything lighter than 40-pound test. Fifty and 60-pound work quite well also. The slight reduction in casting distance these heavier lines may cost you is negligible. Besides, it's depth, not distance that is the primary concern here. In addition, the larger diameter of these heavier lines makes it easier to strike and set the hook in the fish even in the depths.

I'm not sure why, but one place where you seem to stand the best chance of casting to surface breezing yellows is Loreto. No doubt, this is one of the reasons why Loreto was Harry's favorite spot for yellowtail. You can get into them all year long starting in December. During the winter months it can get quite windy, but this is also the time of year for the bigger yellows over the 30-pound mark. Two of the current world record yellows on fly (32 pounds, 8 ounces and 32 pounds) were taken here during the month of March.

Yellowtail get top billing at Loreto, but the region can also produce some excellent fishing for cabrilla, roosterfish,

The roosterfish is a customized version of the jack family.

Even on heavier class fly tackle, roosterfish like this are worthy adversaries.

of politely laughing at me. At any rate, after that particular outing he had great respect for fly tackle and what it could accomplish with these tenacious rock dwellers.

The most consistent action on cabrilla will be had fishing streamers on fast-sinking lines. Weighted patterns like the Clouser Minnow are especially effective. This particular pattern has two important qualities for cabrilla fishing. First, the weighted dumbbell eyes up front give the fly a jigging action when you pause after each line strip. This really seems to turn cabrilla on. I've found that for most situations, 8/32 ounce eyes work best in helping the fly sink in strong running tidal rips which are favorite cabrilla haunts. Secondly, the fact that the Clouser rides with the hook point facing up is a real advantage in this type of fishing because you are constantly working the fly over rocks and reefs. Occasionally you will catch bottom or hang up on a rock, but much less so than you would if the hook point were facing down. Color doesn't seem to be critical as far as cabrilla are concerned although I seem to draw more strikes on dark shades like green and black. The flies can be three to four inches long, tied on hook sizes 1/0 to 3/0.

Most of the cabrilla you can expect to catch on fly will be of the variety known as cabrilla pinto, or leopard grouper. These fish can grow to 20 pounds or more, but most of the ones you're likely to catch are in the three- to six-pound class.

Regardless of their size, all cabrilla will confront you with a tug-of-war contest where you'll generally have to play the fish primarily by hand-stripping the line. In this respect, cabrilla fishing is very similar to what we depicted for calicos.

They both inhabit rock-strewn structure and if they get their way, they will more than likely cut you off.

Cabrilla can be found throughout the year in many spots in the Sea of Cortez, but the most consistent action for fly fishermen is the Midriff area April through November. There are places you can catch them casting from shore, but to really get into them you'll need a boat. Many of the rocks and boulders that are swept by tidal currents (these are referred to as "boilers") are out of range of shore casters. However, even with a boat, experienced boat handling skills are critical when casting to tidal rips around rocks both from the standpoint of fishing success as well as safety. If you have not done this before or are unfamiliar with the area, I strongly recommend hiring a guide who has the expertise.

Tidal surges on incoming tides mean fast-moving water. Baitfish are pushed into pockets and a variety of marine organisms are swept from the rocks. Consequently, it is during these periods that cabrilla will do most of their feeding. To take full advantage of this however, requires proper boat handling and good casting technique. As with any fish that is structure oriented, it is important to get the fly in tight to the rocks. To concentrate on your casting, it's best to have someone else maneuver the boat. Casting distance is important here because the longer the cast you can make, the further away the boat can be positioned from potentially dangerous water.

Though it's not consistently productive, some of the most exciting cabrilla action can be had on poppers cast into the tidal rips. Because there is considerable water turbulence, the popper should be one that will push a lot of water and create a lot of commotion of its own. The 3/4-inch diameter, soft-bodied type with a hole pre-drilled through the center work great for this. They are available from Seattle Saltwater, (206) 283-3590. When cabrilla come up for a popper like this, they do so with a very nasty attitude and the strike is really explosive. Because it's a surface take, you have a better chance of keeping them from getting down in the rocks, but you cannot relax. As soon as they feel the hook and realize they've eaten the wrong offering, they're to going to dive down and head for the safety of the rocks.

Cabrilla may be tough customers, but pargo are the real bad guys of the neighborhood. They have a reputation for humbling those who fish for them with conventional tackle, so when using fly gear, don't get your hopes up too high. The pargo is one formidable adversary. Their reputation is well deserved and they have the goods to back it up. They are a broad-shouldered species with an oversize head that comes equipped with sharp, canine-like teeth. It's these dentures that have given rise to their nickname, dog snapper. They frequent many of the rock-infested areas that cabrilla call home, only when pargo arrive, they often do so in fairly large schools.

Spring and summer months are the best times to find them travelling from reef to reef foraging for baitfish. They'll eat practically anything, but sardinas are their favorite food. There are numerous productive spots for pargo but many of them are unnamed. Some of the spots that you can at least identify on a map are places like Isla Cerralvo (especially the southwestern end of the island), Punta Arena, Punta Perico, Punta Pescadero, the reefs at Los Frailes and the Gordo Banks outside of San Jose del Cabo.

As is true with cabrilla, the depths in which pargo often suspend are well within reach of fly fishermen using fast-sinking shooting lines. Fifteen to 30 feet is the general range and you may not even have to go that deep if you tease them to the surface by slow trolling a live bait. The best places to do this are alongside reefs. Look for dark patches of water and then put the boat in gear so that it barely makes headway. As much as anything, this slow forward movement enables the hookless bait to swim in a natural manner without spinning.

Much like roosterfish, pargo do not linger long after they make a pass at the bait. If you can slap the fly on the water the instant the bait is yanked away, there's a good chance the pargo will strike. That's where your problems begin. Consider that serious pargo fishermen, using stout conventional tackle, spool their reels with 80- to 100-pound test mono and you have some idea of what your prospects are with a 20-pound test class tippet.

You should use a shock tippet for pargo. Fifty-pound test is generally adequate for fish up to 20 pounds. I don't know of any pargo over 15 pounds that have been taken on fly tackle down here. The flies themselves do not have to be elaborate. Just make sure you tie them on strong hooks like the Daiichi 2546, size 6/0. Patterns like the Cotton Candy that resemble the size of the baitfish being trolled will get the pargo's attention. I also like to fish these flies on sinking lines. The only problem is that inevitably you are going to lose a few. You are bound to hang up on the reef or rocks, and when pargo strike a fly, they usually end up owning it.

The Ultimate Inshore Prize: Roosterfish

There is no doubt that the most prized inshore species for the Baja-bound fly fisher is the roosterfish. Its scientific nomenclature has the tongue twisting Latin designation, *Nematistius pectoralis*. In Spanish it is commonly referred to as pez gallo, papagallo, or simply gallo (rooster). It's a member of the jack family, but I like to think of them as souped-up versions. If you have connected with one, I'm sure you'll agree. All jacks are worthy adversaries—they typically hit hard, they take both poppers and streamers, they make strong, fast runs, and they use their slab-sided bodies to make you work for every inch of line. Roosters are no exception.

They not only play the part, they also have the looks to complement their turbo-charged personalities. Their high stacked dorsal fin sports seven elongated flexible spines that raise when the fish is aroused. There is nothing quite like it and when you see these projections suddenly pop from the surface as the rooster comes homing-in on your offering, it's an adrenaline pumping experience in its own right. The resemblance of these spines to a rooster's comb is very similar and I guess that is how the fish got its name. Their coloration is not the sort of artist palate, multi-hued arrangement you find on dorados. Instead, they have a series of dark, bluish black bands. A pair of these run diagonally across their side all the way to the prominently forked tail, not unlike the racing stripes painted on tricked out sports cars.

Roosterfish inhabit tropical seas, their range being confined primarily to the Eastern Pacific. Not a great deal is known about their breeding habits. To date, the few tagging studies that have been conducted seem to indicate that they spawn off Costa Rica about mid-July. The best months to pursue them in Baja is warm weather time, June through August.

Much like dorado, roosters show a wide variation in size. Particularly off the beaches from Loreto south to Cabo San Lucas (this is the primary region for roosters in Baja), it's not uncommon to find junior-class fish going from two to 12 pounds. Larger roosters are occasionally caught from the beach but generally you are better off working from a boat. In water that may only be a few hundred feet from shore you can get into the middle-weight division (20- to 40-pounders) and maybe even get lucky and run into the heavyweights that can hit the scales at better than 60 pounds.

My first encounter with roosterfish on the fly goes back about 26 years. I made a non-stop, 17-hour drive to Mulege where I spent a few days donating flies and considerable tippet material to yellowtail. I managed to land a few and was anxious to move on southward in search of other quarry. Roosterfish were my top priority. Harry Kime told me stories about roosters further south, along the East Cape and I couldn't wait to give them a try.

The conventional wisdom back then was that roosters didn't take artificials. Fortunately, I had a few older friends who regularly fished Baja way before the highway was in and they had taken roosterfish on metal jigs. They were the only ones who didn't laugh when I expressed a desire to try flies. Besides, Harry had pictures of some his catches, so I knew it could be done.

Boosted by this background information I made another grueling, non-stop excursion further south and pulled into a spot called Punta Coyote (I didn't see any but you could sure hear their howls at night) not far from La Paz. I had a car-top aluminum skiff but as I awoke at dawn I could see tiny bait-fish dimpling the surface only about 50 feet from where I was standing. Not wanting to take the time to get the boat ready, I started to rig my 10-weight rod and began to fumble a bit when I heard those sloshing sounds, a sure indication that bigger fish were in the area feeding on bait. I couldn't tell exactly what type of bait it was so I tied on the best generic simulator I had, a small blue and white Deceiver.

They say good things come in threes. In this case, it was the third cast. I had a solid take. About 12 feet of running line shot up from the stripping basket and line began to zip off an old, double-handed Salmon model Seamaster that I was using at the time. In the pre-dawn light it was difficult to get a clear sighting when the fish broke water but after about 10 exhilarating minutes when I slid the fish up on the sand I was elated with my first rooster on fly. At eight to 10 pounds (I didn't have a hand scale with me) it was in the lightweight division, but even on the 10-weight outfit it felt remarkably strong and on several occasions I had to jog down the beach to keep up with it.

As I was soon to learn, this was one of those rare times when it was possible to get roosters to take a fly casting from the beach. They were actively feeding and probably regarded the fly as just another food source. Catching a rooster from the shore is a real thrill, but to enjoy more consistent results, you will want to have access to a boat.

Working from a boat, there are three basic strategies for fly fishing for roosters. Two techniques primarily involve casting, while a third method consists of teasing the fish. When casting to roosterfish, you can toss your flies to classic signs like terrified baitfish busting the surface and other top-water disturbances such as swirls and splashes. Or, you can drift and blind cast in an area that you know is frequented by roosters.

Casting when there is surface commotion is the most exciting because at least you know that game fish are present. If you are running the boat, you have to take care to approach the school of fish carefully. What you don't want to do is charge headlong into the feeding melee. This almost always puts the fish down. The trick is to cut the engine well in advance and try to slide into the periphery of the action as unobtrusively as possible. Often times it's difficult to predict the direction the school may be heading, so sometimes the best course of action is to simply kill the engine, drift along and wait things out. If you have the patience, there are times when the feeding fish will pop up right alongside the boat.

There are some fly fishermen who quit casting when they don't see any apparent signs of fish in the area. If you want to take a break and relax, that's fine. But if you want to maximize your chances of hooking up with a rooster, I recommend that you continue to cast. It can be a tiring process, but it also can be very rewarding. The best day I ever had rooster fishing was the result of blind casting. On a July afternoon, I caught six roosters with a constant barrage of casts close to shore near the little town of La Ribera. Naturally, you don't want to blind cast in just any spot. This particular stretch of shoreline is known to be frequented by roosterfish so I figured that I wouldn't be completely wasting my time tossing flies to barren water.

In an effort to cover as much of the area as possible, I had the skipper move the boat along slowly by putting the engine in and out of gear. To conform to IGFA regulations, I cast and retrieved the fly only when the boat was in neutral. There were pelicans in the area, but they weren't crashing on any bait and there were no apparent signs of any fish. Nevertheless, every half hour or so I could see the telltale dark shape cutting through the water as it tracked my fly. There were some refusals, but six roosters in a three-hour period is fantastic fishing by any standards.

Basically, there are two methods of teasing roosterfish. Each has proved successful and both have their devotees. One method consists of trolling a hookless teaser chugger on a conventional rod and reel setup about 50 feet behind the stern. Usually this is done just a few hundred feet from shore. When a rooster comes up to the teaser, the skipper or mate begins retrieving it with two objectives in mind. First, you want to get the rooster excited. Secondly, you want it to begin tracking the teaser to the point where it swims to within casting range of the angler. When the rooster is aroused and within range, the engine is taken out of gear and the angler makes a cast with a popper pattern immediately behind the teaser. Traditionally, poppers were made from cork, but today most of the bugs are constructed of closed cell Styrofoam. EdgeWater and Seattle Saltwater both make excellent poppers for this. An ideal size is one that is 1 3/4 inches long with a 3/4-inch diameter face. A number of fly fishermen are sold on yellow as the most effective color, but it has been my experience that the commotion on the surface is far more important in getting the rooster's attention.

Strip baits are also used as teasers but I have found that roosters are not overly fond of them. Instead, there is a much more effective method which is based on the premise that roosters prefer live bait to anything else. It makes sense, therefore, to try and entice them with the real thing. Ladyfish, mackerel, and mullet are some of their favorite food sources, but like most saltwater game fish, roosters are opportunistic feeders and given the chance, they will dine on caballito, goatfish, milkfish, striped grunts and the smaller sardinas that frequent this area. With the exception of the fry-size sardinas, if you can procure them, all these other bait make for enticing live teasers.

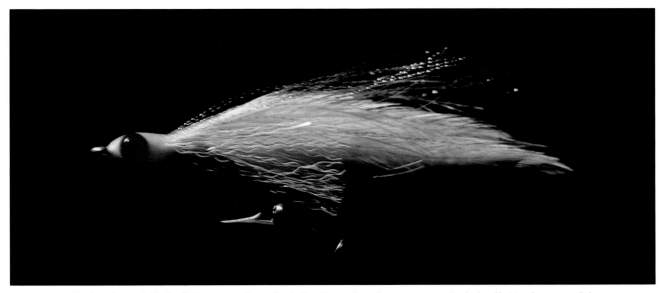

Designed especially for Baja waters, the author's Sardina pattern has proven particularly effective for roosterfish.

As is the case with teasing billfish, teamwork is necessary to pull this off successfully but you have to bear in mind that roosters are more difficult to entice than the former. They will come up for the bait but they don't remain in the area for long. And oftentimes you don't get much forewarning. With marlin and sails, their tall dorsal or long bill are often plainly visible before the fish slashes at the teaser. By keeping a sharp eye you can sometimes spot the rooster's dorsal as it tracks the teaser, but frequently it seems like they just suddenly appear.

Similar to the teasing technique for pargo, the live bait is trolled very slowly. Boats troll differently and you may find that to maintain a slow forward pace, the engine will continuously have to be put in and out of gear. The hookless bait is tethered on a line from a rod and reel combination and allowed to swim relatively unencumbered behind the boat at a distance that is within casting range of the angler. If you drift the bait too far back, not only might it be beyond casting range, you might also lose sight of it. When using a live bait as a teaser, it's important to always maintain visual contact with the bait. If you cannot see what is going on, you may not be able to react quick enough and doing the right thing at precisely the right time is critical when you're trying to tease fish, particularly where roosters are concerned. It is very important for the person manning the teaser to remain constantly alert. When a rooster homes-in on the bait, things happen very quickly. For that reason, the teasing outfit should not be placed in one of the boat's rod holders. It should be handheld. If it's in a rod holder, a rooster can suddenly come up and tear away with the bait before anyone has a chance to react.

This is something you want to avoid. If it swims away with the bait, chances are you will not be able to tease the rooster back to the boat. More times than not, the bait will be badly mangled and the rooster who has just been denied a meal will almost certainly lose interest and vacate the area. Another reason you should closely monitor the bait is that you never know what might come up and try and eat it. One time while drifting a live caballito off Isla Cerralvo, a grouper the size of a 50-gallon drum swam up and sucked in the bait with one quick gulp. My friend who was manning the teaser simply said, "that's Baja".

Incidents like this you can't prevent, but when a rooster comes up for the bait, what you want to try and do is pull the teaser away from the fish before it has the chance to swallow it. The instant the bait is jerked away, the angler should make the cast. Executed properly, I have found that streamers can be every bit as effective as poppers. In that incredibly brief time span of denial, the rooster is thoroughly aroused (perhaps enraged is more accurate). In any case, nature didn't program it to miss many meals. They are ready to pounce on practically any offering that appears edible and for that reason I've found that patterns that simply approximate the size and color of the teaser will rarely draw a refusal. In many cases, it wasn't even necessary to strip the fly any distance because they were on it practically the instant it hit the water.

The size of the outfit you use should be geared to both the size of the fish you expect to encounter and the type of fly or popper you will be casting. You also have to consider the wind factor. Depending on the direction the boat happens to be trolling, you may find yourself in the less than desirable position of having to make a cast directly into the wind. When casts of any appreciable distance have to be made, I like at least a 10-weight rod. For those situations where roosters are being teased, I step up to an 11- or 12-weight rod. To simulate the size of the live bait being trolled, the streamers are large affairs, often over six inches long, and the beefier 11- and 12-weight rods make the delivery much easier.

At both the East Cape and at Cabo San Lucas, it is possible to catch roosters on a year-round basis, but the prime time is generally during summer from June through August. If you take one of these on fly, you'll really have something to crow about.

CHAPTER V

Baja's Bluewater Bonanza

Of all the fisheries we have discussed thus far, Baja remains best known for its incredible big game fishing. The area is a haven for all the major bluewater species. It is believed by some experts in the field that the bluewater big boys migrate from the Pacific, possibly from Hawaiian waters, round the tip of the peninsula, and swim up into the Sea of Cortez. From an area extending just south of La Paz at Punta Arena de Ventana, right to the tip at Los Cabos, marlin, mostly in the form of stripes, dorado, wahoo and yellowfin tuna can be caught all year round. Blue and black marlin and sailfish tend to be more seasonal, with the hottest action coinciding with the warmest temperatures from the end of June to about mid-October.

Because of its location at the tip of Baja where the Pacific meets the Sea of Cortez, at Cabo there always seems to be a population of marlin on hand. One school may be migrating into the gulf, while another may be on its way out.

For the fly fisherman who wants to pursue big game, the areas around La Paz, the East Cape and Los Cabos are a veritable horn of plenty. It's no coincidence that early pioneers with fly gear in bluewater like the late Doc Robinson and Harry Kime, had some of their most memorable experiences in Baja waters. Back in 1962, Robinson took the first striped marlin on a fly in Baja. During that same decade, Harry was getting into sails off Loreto fishing out of pangas.

These areas are also the most developed in terms of facilities geared to the visiting angler. La Paz is the capital and the largest city of Baja California Sur. In the 1950s, sport fishermen from the U.S. began sampling its bounty and a decade later La Paz became world famous as a Mecca for billfish. Angler-based tourism grew rapidly and you'll find a number of

"Charlie", bad boy tuna.

A hooked dorado will often attract other members of its clan.

fine hotels in La Paz such as Los Arcos, Palmiera, La Posada, and the Hotel Gran Baja. But there's a lot more than billfish here. Yellowfin, wahoo, and inshore species like jacks, yellowtail, roosterfish, pargo and pompano offer some outstanding fishing. Nearby Cerralvo Island, the southernmost island in the Sea of Cortez, is also world renown. The island acts as a barrier between Cerralvo Channel and the Sea of Cortez and the variety of game fish in the surrounding waters could fill a marine biology text.

Heading further south, the East Cape also has a long history and excellent reputation for its fishery. The pioneer resort here is Rancho Buena Vista. It's been in operation for over 40 years and continues to offer fine accommodations and excellent service. There are a host of other quality hotels in the area like Spa Buena Vista, Palmas de Cortez, Hotel Playa Hermosa, Punta Colorado, Punta Pescadero, and Rancho Leonero.

Finally, Los Cabos, or The Cape as it's more commonly known, has one of the world's greatest year-round fisheries. Its unique location between two great bodies of water, ensures both a variety and abundance of world class game fish that is difficult to match anywhere. The area also has a number of luxurious hotels. The Hacienda, the Hotel Cabo San Lucas, the Finisterra, Hotel Mar de Cortez, Palmilla Los Cabos, Solmar, Melia Cabo Real and the Twin Dolphin are some of the well known resorts that cater to sport fishermen.

One of the distinct advantages for fly fishermen pursuing bluewater species in Baja, is that for the most part, the fishery is relatively close at hand. You don't need a mega-yacht to get into fish. Of course, you always want to keep an eye out for weather, but for most conditions, small cruisers and even pangas will safely get you to and from the fishing grounds. If it is too rough to go out on these smaller craft, then I don't want to go out at all, regardless of how big the boat is.

The reason big game species are so accessible is that upwellings of nutrient-rich water suspends over sub-marine ledges that drop-off close to shore. In many places, a 10-minute boat ride will put you into classic, ink-blue deep water. The situation is enhanced by Baja's tropical currents that carry bait schools close to the coastline. This explains why you can sometimes run into dorado, tuna and wahoo only a few hundred yards off the beach.

All of the species I am about to discuss are also found on the Pacific side, but much of this is not Baja-based and remains largely inaccessible. To fish any distance from the Cape on the Pacific side, you are basically limited to two alternatives. Either you have access to a large, ocean-going sportfisher, or you make a long-range trip out of San Diego. You can learn more about this type of fishing in Trey Combs' excellent book, *Bluewater Fly Fishing.*

My discussion focuses on the fishing that originates in Baja. The three primary regions are the areas off La Paz, the

East Cape and Cabo San Lucas. The major bluewater species that roam these waters and can be taken by fly fishermen are dorado, billfish (sails and marlin), wahoo and yellowfin tuna. We'll look at each of these separately.

Dorado

Perhaps more than any other species, the dorado has been a staple of Baja ever since sportsmen first began to fish here. As a game fish, they have just about everything you could ask for. I give them a "double A" rating because they are generally abundant and available. Compared to many other species, they take flies eagerly. When you stick one, they go airborne and give a good account of themselves without punishing you. They are beautiful to behold and they are superb eating.

As unbelievable as it may seem, there are some jaded types who consider dorado a nuisance. These are usually the big game guys who strap themselves in fighting chairs and hope for the thousand-pounder. As a fly fisherman, I welcome their "pests" as a godsend.

My first fly rod encounter with this acrobat that can take on the illusion of an artist's palate being launched from the surface, also dates back to the late Harry Kime. As only he could, Harry spun wonderful tales of taking dorado on flies down off the East Cape. This really got me fired up and it wasn't long after that I found myself in these same waters prospecting for "Baja gold".

A technique I used back then and one that I haven't deviated much from today, is to troll for dorado with conventional tackle. This wasn't new to me because I had considerable experience with dorado on long-range trips. Trolling on those trips is the primary means of locating dorado. Normally, for the angler using conventional gear, trolling is often both a means and an end in itself. In fly fishing, at least in the classic sense, trolling is strictly a means of finding fish, but it can also play a secondary function of helping to attract free-swimming dorado to the boat. In common with some other game fish, most notably albacore, dorado have the habit of following other members of their group that have been hooked. The way this was explained to me, at least as far as albacore are concerned, is that other members of the school follow the hooked fish in the apparent belief that the struggling member has found a food source. Whatever the reason, allowing a hooked dorado to swim around the boat is an effective way of drawing other fish to within casting range. Perhaps the hooked fish triggers some feeding mechanism, because in almost every instance, its followers will at least make a pass at the fly. In most of these cases they strike it with little hesitation.

On that early outing, when I experienced the first strike after about 20 minutes of trolling, I didn't really enjoy the encounter on the trolling outfit. First off, the outfit was much heavier than what I would normally have used if I were fishing

Dorado this size can often be attracted by slow trolling a hookless live bait.

When aroused, the dorado's pectoral fins glow like neon lights.

dorado exclusively on conventional tackle. This was a 60-pound outfit. Here, the purpose of the trolling gear was not to provide sport. I was using it primarily as a fish-finding tool. Secondly, once a fish was hooked, its function was to enable me to get the fish close to the boat as quickly as possible. Hooking and briefly fighting the fish on the trolling setup was only a prelude to my ultimate objective of taking a dorado on fly. Instead of landing or releasing the fish in the usual manner, I backed off on the drag a bit, engaged the reel's clicker and set the outfit down in my car-top skiff. I didn't even have rod holders at the time.

It doesn't always work according to plan, but I was lucky that first time out because three other dorado followed the fish that was hooked on the trolling outfit. I picked up the fly rod, made a cast, and began stripping line the moment the fly hit the water. At the time, I was using a four-inch, green and white Deceiver which is still one of my favorite patterns for dorado. The cruising dorado were only several feet below the surface. They were plainly visible in the clear, bluewater. Two of them immediately homed-in on the fly. For a brief moment I could see their pectoral fins glow like neon lights. This is always a sure sign that the fish is aroused. Then in a flash, I felt the surge of the strike in my line hand and I was into my first fly rod dorado.

I've been fortunate to have experienced scenes like this many times since that initial encounter and the thrill of a visual strike immediately followed by a series of twisting, airborne gyrations never has diminished. I guess the next best thing to

catching one yourself is being there for someone else's first encounter. Having hosted many seminars in this region has given me the opportunity to share these experiences many times over with fly fishermen who have their first encounters with dorado. That's one of the great things about this fishery, for most situations, it isn't necessary to be an accomplished fly fisherman to get in on the dorado action. In fact, of all the game fish, dorado are the most accessible to fly rodders. In terms of numbers, it is the species most frequently taken on fly in Baja. When the dorado are in and actively feeding, it's not uncommon for anglers who have never caught a saltwater fish on fly before to have landed a half dozen or so in the span of a few hours.

When trolling for dorado that I plan to hook and not land immediately, as is the process described above, I use small skirted lures like Mako jets and JPRs. These are designed to be trolled at fairly high speeds so you can cover a lot of water. If you choose to troll at slower speeds, you can use plugs like Rapalas and L-Jacks. Like many other game fish, dorado are attracted to the boat's wake so the lures should be positioned fairly close to the boat. Three or four wakes behind is about right. I also do not like to troll more than two outfits. If dorado are in the area, that is all you'll need. Additional outfits will just get in the way and increase the likelihood of tangles.

The reason the artificials I troll for dorado are often accompanied with hooks, is that dorado do not respond well to these kinds of teasers. They typically attack a teaser from the side. If it is yanked from them, they seldom come back for

A dorado taken near a shark buoy relatively close to shore.

it. But if they are hooked, at least you can use that one fish to possibly attract others that may be close by.

When artificial lures fail to raise any dorado, I like to switch tactics and troll a live bait using the same technique that was described for roosterfish. My two favorite baits for this are mackerel and caballito because both are hardy and remain lively for most of the day's fishing. You can try to catch these on your own using special bait ganions, but a much easier way is to buy them from one of the local live bait operations that routinely serve the sport fishing fleets. I like to use a 40- or 50-pound class conventional outfit for this type of teasing.

With a bait needle, run the mono line coming directly from the rod tip through the membrane area immediately in front of the bait's eyes. Tie the line off using a uni-knot. This will create a loop that enables the hookless bait to swim relatively unencumbered. When you reach an area you think might hold dorado, drift the bait behind the boat. Make sure the bait is visible because you will have to monitor it constantly. If you get a blind strike, chances are the fish will have made off with the bait and it will keep on going. You want to try and prevent this. The object is to tease the fish, not feed it. When a dorado sees the bait, it is usually going to try and eat it so the person on the teasing rod will have to be very alert to take it away before this happens. As soon as the bait is jerked from the fish, the boat is taken out of gear and the angler casts the fly.

Admittedly, there are not many anglers who use this approach but it has proved successful for me many times when there was no action on the artificials. It's true that the distances covered are not as great as those achieved with faster trolling speeds, but even with the boat barely making headway, you're still covering a lot of water. And if any fish are in the area, a live offering is more likely to get their attention than an artificial. In addition, the trolling process is simplified. The live bait is already in position and you don't have to worry about clearing other lines before the angler makes the cast. Therefore the cast can be made with little delay, and the quicker the fly can be substituted for the teaser, the better the chances of getting fish to strike. There is no hook in the bait so there is no hassle in trying to release a fish you do not choose to keep.

The dorado's habit of striking their prey from the side is one reason I like to use tandem hooks on the larger flies. Just like the situation with an artificial teaser, if you fail to hook the dorado the first time it strikes the fly, chances are it will not bother going after it again.

Aside from trolling, there are chumming strategies that can be productive with dorado. As with all game fish, far and away the best chum is live chum. In Baja, if you know how to use a throw net you can catch your own. But even if you are proficient with the net, this can involve considerable time so I recommend the easier alternative of purchasing it directly from one of the suppliers. On the East Cape, live bait is primarily in the form of sardinas which is fine because everything dines on them.

Once the bait is taken on board and stored in a live well, the skipper will head for an area that dorado are known to frequent. One of the keys to locating productive dorado grounds is reliance on the dorado's penchant for milling around floating objects. On the Pacific side, floating patches of kelp that have broken away from large inshore kelp beds, (these are referred to as paddies) are favorite holding stations for dorado. In the Sea of Cortez, instead of kelp, the vegetation is more likely in the form of sargasso grass. However, dorado will suspend over practically anything that floats. Logs, driftwood, pieces of cardboard and newspaper, dead sea turtles, birds and even whale carcasses. For a solid week in July a few seasons back, the sport fishing fleets from the East Cape resorts had wide open dorado fishing courtesy of a whale carcass that was floating about 10 miles offshore. The carcass didn't drift too far, so it was almost like a piece of stationary structure, that the boats could run to every day and find fish. Shark buoys are about the only floating objects you might regard as stationary structure and if dorado are in the area, there's always at least a 50 percent chance that some of them will be milling around the buoys. The sport boats from resorts like Rancho Buena Vista, Spa Buena Vista, Rancho Leonero, and Palmas de Cortez frequently make it a practice to test the water around the shark buoys.

However, even if dorado are in the area, some form of chum will normally be required to get them in the mood to take flies. You cannot always depend on this, but there have been times when I would take a skiff out to the buoys and drift near some of the sport boats working the area. In actuality, I was taking advantage of their live chum. There would be so many live sardinas swimming around, that all I had to do was concentrate on casting flies. With all the bait in the water, the dorado are typically in a feeding mode and they'll take flies without much fuss.

Obviously, to draw strikes in a situation like this, your flies should approximate the bait. I've seen folks outfitted with patterns the size of feather dusters become absolutely frustrated because dorado that were plainly visible would not strike their offerings. When dorado are feeding on sardinas, practically any thinly dressed baitfish pattern two to four inches long tied on 1/0 or 2/0 size hooks will get you hooked up.

When using chum, regardless of whether it is live or the chopped-up variety made from squid or larger baitfish like mackerel, bear in mind that the purpose of these handouts is to arouse the dorado, not feed them. Particularly with live chum, I have been in situations where simply too much was being tossed overboard. Not only will your supply be quickly depleted, but if there is an overabundance, dorado (and this applies to other game fish as well) may start keying-in on the chum and ignoring your flies. The trick is to throw out just enough to keep the fish interested. For the most part, skippers and mates on the sport boat fleets are pretty adept at this. However, if you feel that your flies are being ignored because there is too much bait in the water, do not hesitate to say something.

In these waters, bait is a very precious commodity and I don't throw anything away until the fishing trip is over. The live bait wells on the cruisers operating from the hotels do a

A Popovics' Cotton Candy pattern that big dorado find irresistible.

There is no comfort zone when tussling with tuna.

fairly good job of keeping bait alive for most of the day. In the pangas, this is more difficult. Generally the "bait tank" consists of the forward deck area where sea water is provided by means of a bucket. It's primitive, but it gets the job done. Nonetheless, even with the ultra-sophisticated plumbing systems used on some private yachts, bait mortality is inevitable. It's good practice to remove the dead bait from the live well, but do not throw them away. They can be used as chum both whole or chopped up and dorado will respond to both forms.

Dorado have a reputation as being easy to catch and, as a generalization, that's probably true. However, as with all game fish, there are times they can be selective and you will have to make adjustments. One such tactic is a "strip strike" that Harry Kime showed me many years ago. I use it for those times when the dorado seem to want a very fast moving offering. The technique is a simple one of sweeping the rod sideways while simultaneously making a long, sharp strip with the line. The distance you can actually move the fly is limited to several feet at best, but that's often all it takes to entice a dorado into striking the fly.

Very different from this, is a situation where dorado are milling around, picking off bait in a sort of casual manner but, for the most part, ignoring flies. This seems to happen when all you have left for chum are dead sardinas. When these are floating practically right on the surface, dorado will often come by at a leisurely pace and pick them off. Under circumstances like this, burning the fly through the water may not draw any strikes. When this happens, I will have the mate stop chumming. Allow the dorado to eat the remainder of dead

baits in the water and then have the mate resume chumming by throwing only one bait at a time. Try to smack the surface with the bait. The slight noise helps to draw the dorado's attention. Usually a fish will swim by and pick off the dead bait. Repeat this process several times until you feel that the dorado has established a pattern of swimming by and engulfing the bait. Then hold off with the chum, and slap your fly on the water. Many times this is all it takes to draw a dorado to the fly. It sees it lying on the surface just like the other baits it's been feeding on and it will probably try and eat it too.

Generally, I do not use shock leaders for dorado. Especially during those times when they become selective, tying the fly directly to the class tippet seems to draw more strikes. They have needle-like teeth on their tongue and palate and a single row of teeth on the lower and upper jaw, so you are bound to lose a few if they take the fly deeply. However, when dorado are being teased with a live bait like a mackerel, a shock leader can be advantageous. First off, when teased in this manner, dorado are generally much more aggressive and not the least bit leader shy. Many times I've taken them on billfish leaders that were tied with 150-pound test shock tippets. Secondly, this method often produces larger fish, and the teeth on a big bull can easily wear through a light class tippet. A 50- to 60-pound test shock leader will provide ample protection.

One of my favorite patterns when trying to simulate a large trolling artificial or live bait teaser, is Bob Popovics' Cotton Candy. Adhering to the age-old dictum that advises, "big flies for big fish", Bob originally developed the fly for lunker striped bass in his home waters off the Jersey shore. But as he found out on his first trip to Baja not long ago, the Candy does indeed perform according to its namesake for a variety of game fish down here. For the past year and a half, it has been my number one pattern for billfish. "Bull"-size dorado over the 20-pound mark also frequent the same waters as sailfish and striped marlin. For that reason, even when billfish are my primary objective, I always have another outfit rigged with a Cotton Candy that I can cast in the event a big dorado attacks one of the teasers.

The fly works like a proverbial charm and given its unique qualities, I wasn't too surprised at that when I first started using it down here. The body and tail section is tied with a material marketed as Big Fly Fiber. The head portion consists of silicone-treated sheep fleece. The Big Fly Fiber gives the fly the necessary body configuration to effectively simulate large baitfish like mackerel and mullet, and it does so with a minimum of weight. The siliconed head enables the fly to push a lot of water and remain semi-buoyant for a short time even when fished on fast-sinking lines. Due to its minimum weight and ability to shed water like a squeegee, for its size, the Candy is not difficult to cast. It is one of the few flies that draws enthusiastic approval from most of the Mexican skippers and deckhands. At about a foot or so in length (you can tie these even longer), they haven't seen many flies this size

and it elicits a sort of confidence that bluewater game fish will go for it.

Ironically, the first time Bob saw a big dorado engulf a Cotton Candy, he was the one with the video camera, not the fly rod. I was slow trolling a live mackerel for a young fellow who was on his first saltwater fly outing. A large bull swam by and attacked the mackerel with such force that it tore it free from the bridle before I could pull it away from him. Apparently, this tasted good and the dorado wanted more. The boat was out of gear and still sliding forward when I told the fellow to cast the fly. He made a good presentation and the dorado was on it instantly. Unfortunately, in his excitement, the lad had a death grip on the line and as the dorado started to bolt away with the fly, we heard a sickening snap that signals a major malfunction. The kid had big, strong hands and when he failed to allow any line to slip through, the 20-pound tippet parted like fly tying thread. There's a nice big Cotton Candy somewhere out there.

Big game, conventional gear fishermen, for whom dorado often represent an incidental catch, tend to devalue them, in large part because even big "bulls" are fairly easy to subdue on such stout tackle. However, even with fly gear, to maximize the fighting experience, the outfit should be matched to the size of the dorado. These fish can range in size from three- to five-pound juveniles, all the way up to "bulls" that can top the

A 30-pound class yellowfin will give you a good workout.

Yellowfin tearing into baitfish on the surface.

50-pound mark. To date, the largest one taken on IGFA regulation fly tackle is 58 pounds.

Given the fact that even pint-sized dorado will eat streamers over four inches long and nail nickel-diameter poppers, an 8- or 9-weight outfit is about the lightest I recommend. For medium size fish up to about 20 or 25 pounds, a 10- or 11-weight is a good choice. When the fish start topping the 30-pound mark, you should consider one of the billfish-size outfits like a 12- or 13-weight.

In any case, when you go for the "Baja gold" on the fly, you're sure to have a ball.

Wahoo

Back in 1985 when I wrote my first book on long-range fishing, *Hot Rail*, I characterized the wahoo as follows:

> I'm not sure how this wolf of the sea got its name, but it very well could have had something to do with what the first person to have ever hooked one probably shouted in feeling that first scorching run. The latin name is *Acanthocybium solandri*, but it's much easier to shout "wahoo" when you're on.

Even back then I had plenty of experience with these torpedo shaped speedsters, but it was all confined to conventional tackle. The most fun was tossing and retrieving metal jigs which the wahoo hit with a fury unmatched by other species. They would rip off line so fast that when they turned, it actually created a roostertail effect in the water. Many times you could tell someone on deck was hooked up just by the hissing sound of the line slicing through the water.

My first encounter with these fish on fly tackle was on a long-range trip about 19 years ago. I was the only one using a fly rod which was still regarded as a novelty for this kind of fishing. It also made me the object of a lot of friendly ridicule. Nonetheless, everyone was interested in this "trout tackle" and they were anxious to see what I could do with it. Obviously on a boat with 20 other anglers, all of whom are using conventional tackle, the opportunities to fly fish are quite limited. However, for the most part they were a good natured bunch and on one of the trolling rotations where I relinquished my turn with the conventional outfit, they agreed to let me have the port corner with the fly rod where my casting would be less restricted. Taking advantage of the four other trolling rigs that were in the water, I borrowed a standard technique that I used for years as a jig fisherman.

Trolling is the principal method of intercepting wahoo on long-range trips. Anglers take turns trolling off the stern. Whenever a fish is hooked on a trolling outfit, the boat's engines are put in neutral, the other trolling lines are cleared, and the deckhand will give the OK for the remainder of the anglers to begin casting jigs or bait for whatever fish may be in the area. The long-range boats are large, and even with the engines out of gear, they will slide a considerable distance forward before coming to rest. This forward motion can be used to good advantage particularly with wahoo because they generally prefer a fast-moving lure. The jig hits the water, you allow it to sink below the surface, and then you begin retrieving it as fast as you can turn the reel handle. The boat's forward motion increases the jig's speed through the water and wahoo love this kind of action. I have seen them jump out of the water several feet and then actually "dive bomb" on the lure. The skipper and deckhands would always caution you to be extra careful when the jig was close to the boat because they didn't want a free-swimming wahoo suddenly landing on deck. They are wild critters.

We were trolling near Socorro Island, part of the Revillagigedo Island chain, approximately 1,000 miles south of the border. The lure on the starboard corner which was only about two wakes back got bit. This is common because wahoo are attracted by the turbulence of the boat's wake, and often it is the lure that is closest to the boat that gets struck most often. I waited for the deckhand's signal and then shot about a 50-foot cast with a lead-core shooting head.

Once again, I drew from my prior experience with conventional gear which taught me that with trolling feathers, wahoo prefer dark colors like purple, black, green and pink. I had tied on a simple black and purple streamer with a few strands of silver Mylar on the sides.

After the cast, I waited for a mental count of 20 before I began retrieving the line because I wanted the fly to slip below the surface. At the time, I believe Stu Apte was one of the few anglers to have taken wahoo on fly and I really wanted to be part of that elite group. Well, that was my first chance. To my great surprise, and everyone else's onboard, a wahoo clamped down on my fly. I think I only made about four or five strips, when the line suddenly came tight. Needless to say, I was

strand and it was new, to this day I cannot explain why it broke. I prefer single strand wire over the braided kind because it has less diameter for a given break strength. Also, I have seen cases where wahoo and sharks have been able to wear through multi-strand wire. However, one disadvantage of single strand wire is that it is more prone to kinking, and if it has a kink, it can easily break. Maybe when the fish jumped, it kinked the wire.

My next encounter with wahoo was under more favorable circumstances, but I was unprepared and once again, came away empty-handed. I was fishing from a panga off Isla Cerralvo. School size yellowfin were in the area and they were my target. A friend was trolling a big Rapala plug that the yellowfin found quite appetizing. By 9:00 a.m. he already had three. On his next strike, I made the usual cast with the boat in neutral and got struck as the fly was sinking. It was fast, it was subtle, and it was gone. About 10 minutes later when my friend had his wahoo close to the boat, I knew what it was that struck the fly. I

Yellowfin often swim with spinner porpoise.

ecstatic and I can remember everyone cheering. Unfortunately the jubilation was short lived. The fish made one spectacular jump, landed back in the water, and burned off line like I was hooked to an ocean racer. Then the line went slack. For a moment I thought the fish had changed direction and was bolting for the boat—wahoo have a habit of doing that. I reeled as fast as I could, but the line never came tight again. I had the good sense to use wire, but it parted. It was single

didn't have any wire on because I wasn't expecting wahoo. It bit through the mono shock leader as clean as a high speed scalpel.

I don't think there is anything that swims that has a more effective set of teeth. When they hit a bait like mackerel, the slice is so smooth it looks like it could have been cut by a master sushi chef. The teeth are laterally flattened, cup-like projections that are razor sharp. They're embedded in an extremely strong set of jaws. Unlike other species, the wahoo's upper jaw is hinged. That means when they clamp down on something, they usually own it. They also have a hard, bony mouth, and for that reason, I don't like to use big hooks because their corresponding large diameter makes it difficult to get good penetration. A 3/0 to 5/0 hook is all you'll need.

I had to wait another six years before I took one of these sea-going chainsaws on fly and I had to travel all the way to Costa Rica's Canos Island to do it.

A return trip to Isla Cerralvo accounted for my second wahoo on fly where I learned that short shooting heads can help shift the odds in your favor. In the section on leaders in Chapter I, I stated that wire leaders shouldn't be more than about five inches in length if you expect to turn the fly over on the cast. Unfortunately, this length doesn't give you much protection when fishing wahoo. There were a number of times in my conventional tackle days, when wahoo bit past the foot-long wire traces that I was using to connect the jigs. So now, when wahoo are my primary target, I try to use the longest length of wire I can and still conform to IGFA standards. I've found that you can use about nine inches of wire (27- to 50-pound test wire is recommended) and still turn the fly over, if you cast the fly on a relatively short shooting head. On a 12- to 14-weight rod, a 20-foot shooting head is an ideal set up for wahoo. The shorter length enables you to get the head outside the rod tip quickly and eliminates the need for extra false casts. False casting increases the likelihood of fouling the fly and kinking the wire. While the boat is sliding forward, simply drop the fly overboard and allow the head to play out. With the head outside the rod tip, a single backcast followed by the forward cast is all you need to send the fly on its way.

Wahoo are members of the mackerel family which includes species such as king and spanish mackerel and sierra. They are generally not schooling fish, but instead tend to travel in small groups that are appropriately nicknamed "wolf packs". This probably accounts for the fact that the majority of the time they represent an incidental catch for sport fishermen.

If there were personality profiles for game fish, wahoo would definitely be "Type A". They would seldom have to visit a weight clinic either because, like tuna, they are constantly on the move. Their acceleration times are phenomenal. I would win drag races with cars that were half as fast.

In Baja waters, wahoo are found on both sides of the peninsula with the larger ones frequenting the waters in the Pacific. Out here, there are fish that go well over the 100-pound mark. Most of the wahoo in the Sea of Cortez average between 20 and 50 pounds.

Their range in the gulf extends from La Paz, south to San Jose del Cabo. In the northernmost part of this region, wahoo can be taken from about mid-April through October. Late summer and early fall are the peak months. During the winter season, the most consistent action is further south around Isla Cerralvo and the underwater banks outside Cabo San Lucas.

Isla Cerralvo is a popular spot for the small boater because it isn't difficult to reach and its waters are teeming with fish. Deep underwater canyons run the entire length of its eastern shore. At the southeast corner of the island, there are pinnacles that rise to within 75 feet of the surface. When the currents collide with these plateaus, (commonly referred to as "high spots") upwellings of nutrient-rich water are created which establishes an ecological chain. Small baitfish and squid come to forage in the rips and, as always, these are inevitably followed by larger predators which come to feed on them. The wahoo have to share this dining experience with other guests like dorado, sailfish, striped marlin, and yellowfin tuna.

Like their open water companions, wahoo tend to forage around submerged pinnacles. Unless you have intimate knowledge of the area, depth finders and similar electronic aides are invaluable for pinpointing these high spots. The areas where these predominate around the East Cape are the southeast corner of Cerralvo Island (Roca Montana), the inner and outer Gordo Banks east of San Jose del Cabo, and the area between Cabo Pulmo and Punta Los Frailles. On the Pacific side just around the corner from the Cape, you'll find this underwater structure at the Jaime and Golden Gate Banks.

As with most other offshore game fish, seldom will you have the opportunity to cast to a free-swimming wahoo. Trolling is the way to find them and the best time to do this is early morning when the wahoo are most active. Since most of the boats chartered from the resorts do not leave the dock until sometime around 8:00 a.m. the private boater can be at a definite advantage by leaving well before that when it's still almost dark. Some of the best fly rod action occurs from first light to about 7:30 a.m. This is when you want to be out on the fishing grounds.

Just one look at them, and you know that wahoo are built for speed. Accordingly, and this depends of course on the boat, five to 10 knots is a good trolling speed for wahoo. One thing for sure, at this pace you'll be able to cover a lot of areas.

As with dorado, it is a matter of preference whether or not to troll a hookless teaser. On the Kona jet head and Kona hex head trolling feathers, it's an easy matter to eliminate the hooks. With plugs and lures like the CD 68 Rapala and Marauder Makos, you will have to cut the hooks off. Regardless of what you are trolling, when one of the lures is bit, follow the same procedure as described for the long-range boats.

As the boat slows to a stop and the other lines are cleared, cast the fly and allow it to sink. To help get it down, I like to weight my wahoo flies either with metal dumbbell eyes or lead wire around the shank. If there is live bait onboard, have someone start chumming with it as soon as the boat begins to slow after the trolling strike. Live chum will help attract any wahoo that are prowling in the area.

In the process of making the forward cast, it's good practice not to completely release the line from your hand. If you allow the line to shoot through your fingers, when the fly hits the water you'll have immediate control because a portion of the line will already be in your hand. This is important in wahoo fishing because sometimes they will strike the fly as

A Baja "swordsman of the sea".

soon as it lands on the water. They also have the habit of striking the offering as it sinks.

Believe it not, as ferocious as these fish are, the strike can be subtle and you must be alert for the slightest hesitation in the fly's sink rate. Also, contrary to what you may have heard, it is not necessary to burn the fly through the water to entice a wahoo to strike. It would not be possible to move a fly fast enough to actually prevent a wahoo from intercepting it. Similarly, there isn't any food source that can outrun them. Baitfish certainly will try, but when a wahoo is on their tail, the kill is practically a foregone conclusion. Wahoo are probably instinctively aware of this, so after they hit a baitfish school, they can take their time feeding on the crippled carnage left behind. Apparently a fly slowly slipping below the surface is a good simulation of this event, because wahoo that see it are not shy about hitting it. If you do not get hit on the sink, begin retrieving the fly slowly with brief intermittent pauses. This has produced far better results with wahoo than trying to rip the fly through the water.

If you do get a strike, resist the impulse to yank back violently with your stripping hand. Hold the line until you feel solid resistance and then come back with a short, sharp tug. Wahoo go absolutely wild when they feel the hook and you don't want to be yanking back when they start accelerating in the opposite direction. If this happens, the tippet will part like wet tissue paper.

Have the drag set as light as possible. All you want is enough resistance to prevent the line from back lashing. The wahoo's initial run will be like nothing you have ever experienced. In less time than it takes to read this sentence, 100 feet of line will have disappeared from your spool. Do not apply any additional pressure. Just hang on and enjoy the thrill. If you survive the first couple of runs, the odds of landing your prize rise dramatically in your favor. Like a cheetah running down its prey, wahoo are lightning fast, but they do not have much staying power. They burn up an incredible reserve of energy on the first panic flights and once they settle down, you can begin to work on them. Landing one of these "wild ones" on fly will be one of your most memorable experiences in the sport.

Yellowfin Tuna

When you study the ocean's food chain, it seems that everything is either feeding or in the process of looking for something to eat. Just being out on the ocean triggers my own preoccupation with food. It was a beautiful summer morning on the East Cape and I was watching Buena Vista grow smaller and smaller as we headed further out to sea. Prior to depar-

Since sails and other billfish are often within a few miles of shore, seaworthy skiffs can be a practical alternative to the larger cruisers.

ture, I filled myself on a delicious, Mexican style breakfast and already I was hungry. One of my friends remarked that if I were a fish, I probably would not make it as far as puberty because I would have eaten something with a hook attached. My reply was, "just hope the fish are as hungry".

There were reports that yellowfin tuna were in an area about 10 miles offshore and we were anxious to get into them with our fly rods. Any time you tangle with tuna, regardless of the tackle, you are in for a tough go. Every member of the tuna family is a "never say die" game fish that will tax you and your tackle to the very limit. On fly gear, the game can take on grueling dimensions. This is not delicate fishing by any means. As an angler, you should be physically fit because any tuna you tangle with sure as hell will be. As I wrote almost 20 years ago in one of my first articles on the subject, "there is no such thing as an out-of-shape tuna". When one of these beer barrelled dynamos hits your fly at full speed, get set for a back-breaking, arm-wrenching contest that few other fish can match. I've been told many times by friends who have caught both that, with the exception of broadbill swordfish, there is nothing in the sea that can pull as hard and as relentlessly as a tuna. Let's take a brief look at what makes "Charlie" such a bad boy.

According to marine biologists, tuna are very highly evolved. They represent the peak of hydrodynamic refinement. In simple terms, they are very powerful, fast swimmers,

equally adept at both quick-fire sprints and long-haul marathons. When swimming along at a good clip, their streamline shape is maintained as the fins retract into grooves. Even the non-protruding eyes form a smooth, continuous surface with the rest of the body. It's no surprise then, that along with billfish, they rank as some of the fastest swimmers in the sea. In fact, they never stop swimming because they depend on their own forward motion to provide oxygenated water over their gills.

Tuna are negatively buoyant in water. If they stop swimming, they sink. Even during their slowest movement, they must travel a distance equal to their length every second. For some of the larger specimens, this would amount to a rate greatly surpassing the capability of the fastest human swimmers and the tuna would only be loafing along. As you can imagine, their energy demands are very high and some species consume as much as 25 percent of their body weight every day. In the case of yellowfin, few specimens attain a weight over 400 pounds because at this size they simply cannot take in enough nourishment to sustain themselves.

Their growth rate is also remarkable. On the average, during their first year of life, yellowfin weigh about six pounds. They grow to about four times that size in their second year and twelve times their initial weight in their third year. A yellowfin approaching the 400-pound mark would only be about 8 1/2 years old.

So what does all this add up to for the angler who wants to battle them on fly tackle? Quite simply, it means that when one takes your fly, you will be locked on to one of the ocean's toughest adversaries. You won't get spectacular jumps and twisting, turning gyrations characteristic of marine acrobats like billfish and tarpon. Instead, what awaits is one of the most demanding tug-of-wars in the world of sport fishing. When you bury the hook in one, characteristically, tuna take off for the depths. With their compact, muscular, bullet-shaped bodies, they are unmatched when it comes to unyielding staying power.

More so than other game fish, tuna are a "here today, gone tomorrow" type of species. They are found all along Baja's Pacific coast, with the summer months and early fall seeing the most consistent action. In the Sea of Cortez, they range as far north as Bahia de Los Angeles and begin migrating around the Cape up into the gulf around late April or early May. The action can be a hit or miss affair through summer up until late October.

The Pacific side of the peninsula definitely is home to larger yellowfin. The Revillagigedo Archipelago which begins about 220 miles south of the Cape accounts for some of the world's largest yellowfin. Occasionally the gulf side will see some "gorillas" (yellowfin over 100 pounds), but here it's more a matter of quantity. You're more likely to encounter school-size fish in the five- to 20-pound class with occasional 30- to 80-pounders mixed in. Believe me, even a 30-pound yellowfin on a 12- or 14-weight rod can keep you bent over for a good half hour or so.

Since the tuna is an open-water predator programmed to hunt its prey on the move, trolling is the best means of locating roving schools. Generally the same speeds and trolling lures used for wahoo will draw strikes from yellowfin. Zuker and Sevenstrand offer a number of proven artificials for tuna. The 5 3/4- and eight-inch Zuker in zucchini and Mexican flag colors are old reliables, as are the Sevenstrand Tuna Clones. The two-ounce zucchini and red mackerel colors seem to draw more than their share of strikes from yellowfin. What makes this fishery so challenging is that the yellowfin's preferences can change on a day-to-day basis. To successfully draw trolling strikes you have to be willing to experiment. The boat's speed, the distance the lures are trolled behind the boat, and the size and color of the artificals are all variables that have to be constantly manipulated.

Aside from relying on trolling strikes, two other signs you want to be especially alert for are diving birds and schools of spinner porpoise. Bird action we've mentioned before, but in the case of yellowfin, the presence of spinner porpoise is often a sure sign that tuna are in the area. As a commercial fisherman taught me many years ago, yellowfin like to swim with spinner porpoise. Perhaps it has something to do with the fact that porpoise herd schools of bait which the tuna then feed on. But whatever the reason, it's an established fact that yellowfin seem to have a strong affinity only for the spinner porpoise. They avoid other species.

If you see large surface splashes or arching silhouettes off in the distance, it's definitely something to investigate. Just as with a breaking school of fish, do not run into the middle of the school. Instead, try to determine the direction the school is travelling and position the boat so that you can intercept them at the leading edge of the school.

This is the strategy we used that day off the East Cape. Other than the leaping porpoise, we didn't see any surface activity. My friend who was running the boat had a lot of experience with tuna and no one had to tell him how to setup. Once he figured the direction the porpoise were travelling, he opened up the throttles and ran the boat until we were about 150 yards ahead of the pack. He then made a turn so the trolling feathers would swing right by the front of the porpoise school. The action came off just like it had been choreographed. There were three trolling feathers and all of them got struck almost simultaneously. Because the lines had to be cleared, only one of us could cast, and my friend who was first with the fly rod was about to score with his first yellowfin. The boat had almost come to a stop, but I told him to let the fly sink as much as possible. When the angle of the line looked fairly steep, I gave him the OK to start stripping line with a moderately paced retrieve.

Yellowfin, like their close cousins the wahoo, tend to swim mostly in the upper reaches or mixed layer of the ocean which is separated from the deeper, colder water by the thermocline. However, this doesn't mean that you can expect to find them right on the surface. To score with tuna, most of the time you're going to have to get the fly down.

I heard my friend yell before I saw the arch in the rod. The football expression, "down and out" takes on special meaning when you have a yellowfin on the other end of your line. Sometimes smaller tuna will jump when they nail the fly, but even the juveniles do not wear themselves out with aerial displays. Instead, they typically make a long, powerful run and then sound into the depths where you'll have to work hard to recover every inch of line. My buddy was new to the fly rod, but he was an experienced bluewater fisherman and had the gleaming yellowfin boatside in about 20 minutes. Typical of the fish they were catching at the time, we guessed the fish's weight at about 18 pounds.

The next day, we ran into terrified pods of bait that were being harassed on the surface. This time it was my turn with the fly rod and I shot a cast into the middle of the melee. I let the fly sink for a mental count of about 20. Instead of retrieving the fly in the conventional manner, I let it hang in the depths and jigged it by pulling the line back and then allowing it to go forward again. I never let go of the line. About six pulls later, a yellowfin nailed the fly. For the next three hours this fish had my undivided attention. We never saw it because after it sounded, I wasn't able to regain enough line to even bring it to color. When the line finally went slack, I thought the 16-pound class tippet may have broken. The larger yellowfin have teeth that can wear through small diameter line. Normally I use a shock leader of 50- or 60-pound test mono, but at times the tuna are wary and I tie the fly directly to the

*When a billfish jumps, to reduce the strain on the leader,
push the rod toward the fish.*

tag end of the class tippet. At the other end of the spectrum, there are times when you can even use wire leaders and tuna don't seem to mind, but this wasn't the case here. The fish I had on could have been one of the "gorillas" or just an exceptionally powerful member of the middle-weight division. We'll never know because the fly hook eventually pulled out. I still have the fly in my office as a reminder of another humbling experience with yellowfin.

Baja Billfish
In trying to capture the flavor of their sport, over the years billfish devotees have come up with a number of colorful descriptions and analogies. Two that stick in my mind go something like this: "Billfishing means big bills and no fish," and "billfishing is a lot like flying, hours of boredom interrupted by seconds of absolute pandemonium".

Like many characterizations, these are a bit overdrawn, but there is a modicum of truth in what they're saying. In many parts of the world, billfishing is strictly a big bucks pastime. In my home waters off Southern California, fishermen who chase striped marlin can run up five digit fuel bills in the course of a single season. Secondly, as far as the boredom factor is concerned, there can be long periods when nothing is going on. Even in the fish-rich waters of Baja, you cannot expect billfish to be popping up every few minutes.

In this regard, it is interesting that it's seldom mentioned, but one of the qualities that makes for a good billfish angler is a combination of patience and persistence. Ninety-five percent of this game involves trying to locate the fish. This is accomplished by means of trolling, often hour after hour of dragging lures and baits behind the boat. Once the lines are

out, you try to remain constantly alert for any telltale signs, like diving birds, bait spraying out of the water, surface splashes, circling frigates, rip lines and changes in water color. On occasion you might get real lucky and see a sailfish or marlin swimming lazily on the surface. But most of the time, the only sign is the one that suddenly appears when you least expect it. A "swordsman of the sea" comes up behind a teaser. You may have trolled for hours in a rough sea that pounded you like a prizefighter or waited it out with the sun beating down like a giant oven. But when the dorsal fin first breaks water like a submarine's periscope and the bill starts dueling with the teaser, all of that discomfort is suddenly forgotten. The drowsiness is suddenly gone and you get an adrenaline rush that gets you moving like a dragster with a green light.

The first time a participant in one of the Saltwater Challenge events witnessed a scene like this, he simply said, "now I know why people come to Baja". He probably didn't realize it at the time, but he wasn't too far off the mark. From the standpoint of sport fishing and the accompanying boom in tourism, it is billfish that put Baja on the map. The first American sportsmen who visited the area were primarily interested in marlin. Practically everything else was regarded as an incidental catch. Today, of course, that's no longer the case as fishermen the world over come to challenge a stellar lineup of game fish. Nonetheless, top billing still belongs to billfish.

Aside from the fact that Baja boasts one of the world's largest concentrations of billfish, the one quality that makes this fishery so popular is that, for the most part, the fish are readily accessible. The four major factors that attract game fish to a given area are food sources, structure, current and water temperature. Baja is blessed with an abundance of all this in the right combinations and it is all relatively close to shore. The sub-marine canyons, ledges, underwater plateaus and pinnacles are within reach of seaworthy skiffs. This makes Baja one of the few places where the small boater has ready access to the world of big game fishing.

In addition to relatively easy access, the areas around La Paz, the East Cape and Cabo San Lucas offer year-round opportunities for billfish. Like anywhere else however, there are prime times. At La Paz, June through September are the peak months for sails, stripes and blue marlin. On the East Cape, sails predominate during May through December, while striped marlin are more abundant March through December. If you want to try for blues and blacks, June through November is the time. At the Cape, your best shot for any of these billfish is also June through November.

If you are new to the game, the best way to proceed is to charter a boat from one of the resorts. All hotels listed in the beginning of this section have charter fleets. Especially in offshore fishing, when conditions can change on a daily basis, there is no substitute for local knowledge. As far as fly fishing is concerned, even though it is becoming more popular down here, many of the skippers and mates are still primarily tuned-in to conventional tackle methods. Many,

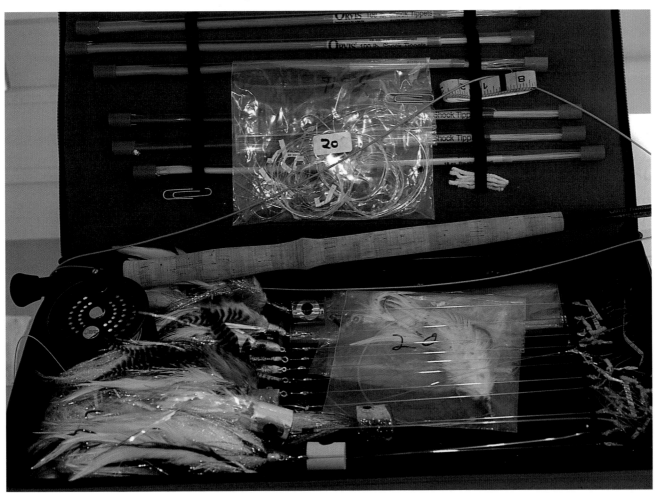

*It's important to keep your billfish flies and leaders
organized and ready to go at a moment's notice.*

however, are willing to learn new methods and make the necessary adjustments. This is important, because regardless of whether you are chartering or running your own boat, there are certain techniques you need to be familiar with to successfully challenge billfish on fly tackle. Let's begin with trolling.

Like other game fish we covered in this section, nature programmed billfish to chase down their prey. So once again, trolling plays a major role in this kind of fishing. Similar to wahoo, billfish prefer offerings that move along at a fairly fast clip, which means that the trolling speed should be somewhere around seven to 10 knots.

As far as selecting trolling lures is concerned, the wide range of styles and colors can be overwhelming. To narrow the choices down somewhat, think in terms of trolling speed. Lures that are designed for high trolling speeds feature conically shaped heads that look like bullets. These often work best in the morning hours when the sea is calm. In contrast, lures that are intended to swim through the water have heads that are slanted or scooped. They are usually a better choice when the sea gets choppy and you have to reduce trolling speed. Whichever you choose, avoid trolling both types of lures at the same time because their action varies according to the boat's speed.

A second choice you have relates to the composition of the lure's head. The more traditional heads are the hard types. In the early years of big game fishing, they were made from lead. This was replaced by pot metal, and today most are constructed of plastic. There are also soft heads made of rubber. A number of fly fishermen prefer these for teasing purposes. The argument is that when a billfish grabs a soft head lure, it will feel more like a natural bait than a hard chunk of plastic and the fish won't reject it as readily.

The colors and combinations of the plastic skirts that trail behind the heads have more variations than a Venice Beach paint shop. Blue/white, white/hot pink, white/hot orange, black/green, black/red, Mexican flag and zucchini color combinations will all raise billfish. The trick is to find the combination that is currently drawing the most attention. If I'm on a charter, I always start out with the skipper's recommendation. If nothing materializes after about an hour or so of trolling, you can always change.

Amidst this array of bewildering choices, there is one fact that you can always rely on. Adding a strip bait to the trolling lure, usually in the form of a dorado or tuna belly, will greatly enhance its effectiveness. This simply works on the principle that there is no substitute for the real thing. It reminds me of the old margarine commercial which admonished us that we "can't fool Mother Nature". To my knowledge, there never have been any experiments studying the taste preferences of billfish, but it makes a lot of sense that holding a real bait in its mouth is a more pleasurable experience than chomping down on a synthetic like plastic or rubber. Conventional tackle, big game fishermen, have known this for a long time, and it was in these circles that the venerable "Panama belly bait" first originated.

Unlike the fleets in many other parts of the world, the charter boats in Baja do not normally have these belly baits readily available. If you want to troll with them, you have to prepare ahead of time. You may find a skipper or mate who is willing to do this for a small fee, but more than likely, you'll probably have to make some up yourself. The first order of business is to visit the resort's fish cleaning area. There are almost always some dorado and tuna that have to be filleted. Ask whoever is assigned the fish cleaning chores to save some bellies for you.

There are a number of ways to prepare these strips for trolling, but essentially they all involve the following steps. First, a teardrop-shaped strip is cut from the belly. Next, using a section of heavy leader material, (either mono or braided wire) roughly half the length of the strip, crimp loops in both ends. Fold the strip over the leader. Using a special bait needle that can be purchased from tackle shops that carry big game gear, stitch the sides of the belly together. Old Dacron line makes good sewing thread for this. To make sure the bait will not be pulled off the leader, take a few stitches through the end loop that is encased in the belly strip. Finish sewing the strip taking extra stitches at the end of the strip so that it tapers slightly. The finished product should look something like a sleek-shaped baitfish. The strip is connected to the trolling outfit by means of a snap swivel that is tied to the tag end of the line coming from the rod tip. The swivel is fastened to the second end loop crimped on the bait's leader. This way, the strip can be fished by itself or inserted through the back end of a plastic trolling skirt.

Ideally, for a full day's fishing I like to have a half dozen of these bellies on ice, rigged and ready to go. If you've done a decent stitching job, the strips will have an enticing swimming motion in the water.

Contrary to the practice of some offshore fly fishermen, I prefer to keep the number of teasers to an absolute minimum. The more lines you have in the water, the greater chance of tangles. Even more critical is the added time it takes to clear these other lines before the fly is cast. As soon as a fish comes up on one of the teasers, it's important to take in the other lines as quickly as possible. If the fish gets frustrated with not being able to capture one teaser, it may turn its attention to another. With too many choices however, the fish may simply lose interest and give up the pursuit altogether. To alleviate these problems, I prefer to troll with only three lines out. If live bait is available, I'll have a fourth outfit tethered to a hookless bait that is kept alive in the bait well.

Because it is difficult for some people to estimate distances in terms of feet, to gauge how far back to place the trolling lures, count the number of waves or wakes formed by the boat's engines. As a general guideline, try staggering the lures at distances that vary from approximately three to six wakes back.

Of course, before the trolling lines are set, you have to decide what type of fly you are going to present. Some fly fishermen prefer poppers while others swear by streamers. There is no doubt that a popper is more effective in getting a billfish's attention because of the surface commotion it creates. The downside, however, is that sometimes it's difficult for a billfish to eat a popper. They swipe at it with their bill and it pops away from them. If they manage to get hold of it, the big foam head can impede hook penetration. You don't have these problems with a streamer, but there are times when billfish won't strike because they're not excited by the fly.

Popovics' Cotton Candy fly that I discussed in the section on dorado, is my first choice for billfish because it incorporates the advantages of both the popper and streamer. The fly's large profile and silicone head will create almost as much disturbance as a big popper. Secondly, the tandem hook arrangement and the separation qualities of the strands of Big Fly Fiber, give this fly a level of hook-setting effectiveness that's equal to any streamer pattern. For the primary hook, I use a Mustad 3407 in a 7/0 or 8/0 size. The tandem hook is an Owner SSW, size 7/0.

Just like people, billfish do not all react the same way. There are differences between species and individual fish as well. It's been well established that sailfish are the easiest of all to tease. Some have characterized them as "dumb and greedy", but too many have foiled my efforts so I don't agree with that description. In comparative terms, sailfish do tend to be less wary than marlin. But these generalizations notwithstanding, you have to be prepared for different reactions. Some fish are very aggressive and they'll follow the teaser almost all the way into the boat's cockpit. Others require skillful coaxing, and you'll have to let them taste the teaser several times before presenting the fly. Most frustrating of all, are the ones that end up teasing you without ever falling for the ruse. They light up, rush the fly and suddenly decide it isn't to their liking. Then they veer off like a spoiled child who is no longer enchanted with its toy.

Bearing these different reaction scenarios in mind, the following steps are proven methods for teasing billfish to the fly. First off, when a fish homes-in on the teaser, let it get a taste of it. This sometimes requires a deft touch because the object is to allow the fish to mouth the bait, not engulf it. The first time a fish grabs it, try and pull the teaser away as gently as possible. If you yank it away too fast, the fish may be discouraged right from the start and figure it's not worth the effort to continue the pursuit. If need be, a second or third taste can be terminated in pull-aways that are progressively

A sailfish in the last stages of struggle.

make a couple of short, sharp jabs. If you use the rod, do not strike upward, because if the fish runs directly to the boat, you won't be able to get the line tight again. Once the fish is solidly on, concentrate on clearing the loose line on deck and getting the fish on the reel. Now you can strike the fish several more times with the rod just to ensure a positive hook set.

The drag setting on the reel should be no more than two to three pounds. With line-burning runs and explosive jumps coupled with violent head shakes, you have to be very careful to avoid break-offs. When the fish is in the water, it cannot shake its head that much, but when it breaks the surface it can really go wild. To reduce the added strain, when the fish jumps, bow to it. This is accomplished by simply pointing the rod directly at the fish while simultaneously bending at your waist.

After it completes its jumping spree, the next step is to try and get fairly close to the fish, to within 100 feet or so. The object is to recover as much line as possible, so when you pump on the down stroke, lower the rod tip right into the water. At this stage of the contest, you are not really taxing the fish. It will be suspended in the depths with its pectoral flared and you will have to maintain constant pressure if you expect to get it coming your way. This is where knowledgeable boat handling really pays dividends. Instead of staying directly over the fish, the boat should move away. In the process more line will come off the reel, but the distance and resulting angle will help coax the fish back to the surface. The captain should also try to keep the fish at about a 30 degree angle to the boat. This way, if the fish turns toward the boat, the captain can quickly veer away from it. In addition, these maneuvers will prevent the leader and line from falling back over the fish's body.

When the fish is near the surface, (you will be able to see color) start pulling the fish low and sideways. This puts pressure on the fish from the underside where it can't use its pectoral fins to advantage. Even though the fish may be close, do not increase the reel's drag setting. If the fish suddenly decides to jump or bolt away, you won't be able to loosen it in time and the leader may break. Instead, maintain pressure with your hands. This way you can react instantaneously if need be.

When the moment of truth arrives and the mate is able to grasp the bill, back off on the drag. With slack in the line, the fly can be removed easily and safely. Unless you think you have a record, the fish should be released but before doing so, it must be revived. All the crews I've ever fished with in Baja know the procedure. For those of you who want to do this on your own, the process is simple. With gloves on your hands, grasp the fish by the bill and hold it alongside the boat. The boat should be moving ahead slowly. It may take a few minutes before the fish has gained sufficient strength to swim away on its own. You will know when it has, because it will begin to struggle a bit. Hold it a few seconds more and then gently release your grip. Hopefully another fly fisherman will be able to challenge it once again on a future outing.

more violent. Hopefully, this will thoroughly enrage the fish. After the final taste, the teaser should be pulled completely out of the water. To do this effectively, point the rod straight at the teaser with the line taut and make a quick upward jerk on the rod to pull the teaser from the fish's mouth. Immediately drop the rod and reel up the slack. Then using the leverage of the rod, swing the teaser up toward the bow of the boat in one continuous, smooth motion. If things go according to plan, the fish reacts like a kid who's just had an ice cream cone yanked from its lips. It probably thinks the bait has jumped out of the water and managed to escape. Almost simultaneous with this feat, the fly is substituted for the teaser. Now the fish thinks the bait has returned to the water and it's ready to pounce on it.

When making the cast, the object is to place the fly about five to six feet to one side of the fish. This way, the fish must turn almost 90 degrees to take the fly, increasing your chance of hooking it in the corner of the mouth. It's very difficult to hook a billfish coming straight at the fly because its beak is very hard. So is the lower lip in front. That's why you want to try to sink the hook in the soft corner.

How you strip the fly depends on the reaction of the fish. Some skippers will advise the angler to just let the fly or popper lie in the water without imparting any stripping action. Often the big fly or popper splashing down on the surface is all it takes to get the fish's attention. At other times, it may be advisable to strip the fly in rapid sequences. If the fish doesn't take on the first or second cast, chances are it will have to be teased once again. That's when I'll drop the live bait in the water. If the fish is still in the area, the bait is sure to get its attention and nothing fires up a billfish like a live bait.

When the fish takes the fly, strip line until you feel solid resistance. I prefer to strike the fish exclusively with my line hand, but there are others who recommend augmenting this by sweeping the rod sideways. To ensure good penetration,

Chapter VI

Baja Travel Tips

For most people, travel to Baja entails either flying or driving. Some folks fly their own aircraft. In fact, it was private pilots who were among the first to fish Baja. Today, commercial airlines provide daily flights from a number of major U.S. cities making air travel the most convenient option.

For those who don't mind spending the extra time, or want to have access to their own boat, driving down is the way to go. Unfortunately, many people are hesitant to do so because of the horror stories regarding bandits and bad roads. Contrary to what you may have heard, there are no Pancho Villa types out there waiting to ambush you as soon as you cross the border. The road does get chewed up, but most of the time it's passable.

It does rain in Baja and this can result in treacherous driving conditions.

Left: Baja is especially tough on tires.

Nonetheless, driving down Mexico Highway 1 does require a good deal of caution and extra preparation. I am especially sensitive to this because in two separate incidents, I lost three friends in driving accidents. One friend died when a pickup truck crossed the road and hit him head on. A few years after that another friend and his wife were killed when their four-wheel-drive went off the road and down an embankment. They were on the way to the spot we call "Variety" near Guerrero Negro. Their daughter and her girlfriend miraculously survived and told us later that my friend had fallen asleep at the wheel. He awoke just as the wheels began to

gives you permit and license information and where you can purchase them.

To be in Mexico, you'll need proof of citizenship such as a passport or birth certificate in order to be issued a tourist card. These forms can be obtained at the border, from travel agents, airline ticket counters or Mexican Consulates in major U.S. cities. If you plan to fish (doesn't everyone) and are 16 years of age or older, a Mexican fishing license is required. The license is included in the price of a trip if you are fishing from a commercial passenger-carrying sport boat in Mexican waters. Otherwise, you have to provide one yourself. They are available from the Mexican Department of Fisheries as well as a number of tackle stores that book trips or outfit anglers for fishing in Mexico.

As for the actual drive itself, I would like to offer the following recommendations. First off, just because you have crossed the border and are free from the close traffic surveillance that is normal in most parts of the U.S., resist the temptation to drive like you were in a *Grand Prix* race. Personally, I love fast sports cars and high speed driving, but this is not the place to do it. A number of signs in Spanish will remind you that this highway was built to further the region's economic development, not for high speed driving and you would be wise to heed this advice. The side of the road is strewn with crosses and shrines in memory of those who were careless and lost their lives.

The highway is narrow, there are blind curves and dips everywhere, there are no retaining walls, and most of the roadway is bordered by open range land with no fences. It's common to come over a rise and suddenly be confronted with farm animals like cows or horses casually meandering about in the middle of the highway. If you're going too fast, you'll never be able to stop in time.

For much the same reason, driving in the dark is not recommended. It's been estimated that 80 percent of the accidents occur at night. The road retains heat and it's common for animals to lay on it at night. This is also the time when big trucks do most of their travelling and they take up a whole lot of roadway.

In the event you run into mechanical problems or experience a breakdown, help will eventually be on its way in the form of the Green Angels (Angeles Verdes). These are specially equipped green utility trucks under the direction of Mexico's Department of Tourism whose job is to provide assistance to stranded motorists. They carry some spare parts but it's good insurance to carry some of this yourself. At the minimum, for your vehicle you should have the following: jack, spare tire (inflated), portable air pump, extra belts, spark plugs and plug wrench, spare motor oil and gasoline and fuel filters. If you are towing a boat, you should carry extra items for the trailer such as wheel bearing grease and grease gun, a spare set of wheel bearings, spare tires, and extra trailer tie downs.

Now all you have to do is proceed carefully, enjoy the scenery and have a safe trip. Adios.

leave the pavement, but it was too late. Prior to this tragedy, my friends and I were always in a hurry to get to our fishing spots. We continued to drive when we were tired and we often drove in the dark. These are bad mistakes and it's just plain luck that we didn't suffer more mishaps.

I don't make the drive as often as I used to, but with over 25 years experience, I've learned a few things (some the hard way) that I would like to pass on.

Aside from having your vehicle in tip top condition, the first thing you want to do is have all the necessary paperwork completed. Before you even cross the border, make sure you have Mexican insurance for your vehicle and boat and trailer if you are towing one. Regardless of what your American policy says, Mexican law only recognizes insurance that is written by licensed Mexican insurance companies and their representatives. If you are taking a boat down, you will also need a Mexican boat permit even for a car-top skiff. These may be obtained by calling the Mexican Department of Fisheries in San Diego (619) 233-6956. You'll get a 24-hour recording that

A
Albright knot, 20
Angler's Guide to Baja California, The, 34
Arizona Fly Fishing Store, 32
B
Baja Anglers, 36
Baja on the Fly, 36
Barnes, Bill, 16
barred perch, 28, 29
Beach Bug, 31
Bend Back Siliclone, 31, 33
billfish, 66
Bimini twist, 16, 17, 19
Bluewater Fly Fishing, 53
bonefish, 34
C
cabrillo, 45
calico bass, 32, 33
Cast, The, 9, 12
Clifford's knot, 22, 23
Clouser Minnow, 12, 31, 32, 33, 34, 39, 48
Combs, Trey, 53
corbina, 29
Cotton Candy, 49, 57, 58, 59, 68
croaker, 29
D
Deceiver, 31, 33, 39, 50, 55
dorado, 8, 53-56,
E
EdgeWater, 50
F
fishing license, Mexican, 71
fly casting, 9
"Fly Casting with Lefty Kreh", 9
fly line, 11, 14, 15
fly reels, 11, 13, 14, 16
fly rods, 11

G
Graham, Gary, 34, 37
Grey, Zane, 8
H
halibut, 30, 31
haywire twist, 23, 24
Hemingway, Ernest, 8
Hot Rail, 60
Huff, Steve, 16, 17, 22
Hufnagle, 20
I
IGFA, 17, 18, 50, 60, 62
insurance, Mexican, 71
J
jack crevalle, 40
Jaworowski, Ed, 9, 12
K
Kime, Harry, 8, 11, 14, 42, 43, 45, 49, 50, 52, 54, 58
Kreh, Lefty, 9, 19, 22, 31
L
ladyfish, 36, 38, 41
leaders, 17
Longfin tackle store, 41
M
Mexico Dept. of Fisheries, 71
Mexico dept. of Tourism, 71
Miller, Tom, 34
N
Napoli, John, 12
needlefish, 38, 43
non-slip mono loop, 22
O
Orvis Guide to Saltwater Fly Fishing, The, 45
P
pargo, 45
permits, boat, Mexican, 71
Playa San Ramon, 30
pompano, 39,

Popovics' 3-D Fly, 39
Popovics, Bob, 31, 32, 57, 58, 59
R
Rancho Soccoro, 30
Reyes, Tony, 41, 45
Robinson, Doc, 9, 52
Rock, Ron, 32
roosterfish, 39, 48, 49
S
sailfish, 69
Saltwater Fly Patterns, 31
Sandcrab Dark, 31
Sandcrab Light, 29, 31
Sardina, 39, 51
Seattle Saltwater, 49, 50
Sevenstrand, 65
sierra, 38
Siliclone, 31
Solis, Jeff, 34
Sosin, Mark, 19, 22
speed nail knot, 20, 23
Spey, rods, 12
Stearns, Bob, 16, 17
stripping baskets, 35
surgeon's knot, 17
surgeon's loop, 21
T
Tijuana, 26, 30, 32
Trilene knot, 21
tuna, yellowfin, 52, 59, 60, 61, 63
U
uni-knot, 21, 56
W
wahoo,
white seabass, 32, 42
Y
yellowtail, 42
Z
Zuker, 65